Praise for *The Sports Parent*

"*The Sports Parent Solution* is a game changer {
alike. Its compelling storytelling, practical soluti...,
examples addressing the challenges of sports parenting set it apart from
the rest. The 'Take Action' sections empower every reader to apply
these skills brilliantly. I wholeheartedly recommend this book, as well
as all of Nerbun's work, for its thoughtful, well-researched topics that
captivate and inspire readers."

Colleen Dawson, William & Mary women's lacrosse

"J.P. is one of those people who not only helps us see leadership in
sports differently, he gives us practical tools and strategies that work!"

**Anson Dorrance, UNC women's soccer, 21 NCAA championships &
1991 Women's World Cup**

"J.P. has been an important voice in coach education and team culture
building for the past decade. He is one of my go-to people in this space.
His new book will help coaches and parents build a relationship based
on trust and mutual respect and help them become allies instead of
adversaries in athlete development. It is time we stopped *dealing* with
parents and started *engaging* them, and this book will teach you how."

John O'Sullivan, Changing the Game Project &
The Way of Champions Podcast

"This approach works! Utilizing relatable stories and straightforward,
proven action steps, J.P. has created yet another brilliant coaching
resource that will enhance your confidence working with parents. A
must-read for any coach seeking methods to leverage relationships with
parents and take the next step toward the future of coaching."

Patrick Quirk, The Hun School boys soccer

"*The Sports Parent Solution* is an inspiring and transformative guide that expertly navigates the intricacies of the parent-coach relationship, providing invaluable insights and actionable strategies for coaches to cultivate growth and facilitate positive change. Through captivating firsthand anecdotes and real-world experiences, this book empowers coaches to approach even the most formidable coaching moments with assurance and sagacity."

Erik Robitaille, Prairie Hockey Academy

"J.P. delivers once again! *The Sports Parent Solution* presents practical strategies and valuable insights to cultivate effective communication and collaboration between coaches and parents. A must-read for anyone in the coaching realm aiming to establish a supportive environment that unleashes the full potential of young athletes."

Mark Cascio, Courtside Consulting

"This is a must-read for coaches at any level! J.P. employs real-life stories and offers practical, easily implementable strategies to dismantle common barriers between coaches and parents, replacing them with strengthened relationships that make parents feel connected and valued. As an added bonus, parents will organically contribute value to your program!"

Sam Klassen, Briercrest College men's hockey

"*The Sports Parent Solution* is a book that all coaches should read. Connecting and aligning with parents in the sports world not only demonstrates mindfulness but also empowers your team to feel more connected."

Josh Strasser, McCutcheon High School football

"J.P. lays out effective methods and strategies that help coaches connect with parents. I have implemented many of these same strategies and tools with my parents, and have seen overwhelmingly positive results. A must-read for any coach who wishes to build positive relationships with parents!"

Tyler Wright, Mt. Zion High School principal

"J.P. has nailed it again! This book helps coaches and leaders build positive relationships with parents, creating an amazing culture within a program and team. Readers gain sound insight into strategies and activities to use before, during, and after the season that are proven effective in building positive relationships and opening communication between parents and coaches. It is a must-read for any coach who truly wants to build a solid and successful culture in their program."

Andy Cerroni, Hamilton High School boys basketball

"*The Sports Parent Solution* is an invaluable guide for coaches seeking effective collaboration with parents. Through insightful stories and practical suggestions, this book not only enriches the player's experience but also strengthens the coach-parent relationship. A must-read for every coach looking to excel."

Nick Pocius, Kasson-Mantorville High School boys basketball

THE
SPORTS
PARENT
SOLUTION

THE

SPORTS
PARENT
SOLUTION

PROVEN STRATEGIES FOR
TRANSFORMING PARENTS FROM
OBSTACLES TO ALLIES

J.P. NERBUN

FOREWORD BY
NATE SANDERSON

Printed in the United States of America.
First edition 2023.

Cover and layout design by G Sharp Design, LLC.
www.gsharpmajor.com

ISBN 979-8-9860912-2-8 (paperback)
ISBN 979-8-9860912-3-5(ebook)

To my children Alena, Kieran, and Conall, who accompanied me during countless early mornings as I wrote this book.

It is my hope that sports will forever enrich and strengthen the bond between us.

CONTENTS

FOREWORD

At the end of another long day of teaching, my principal walked unexpectedly into my classroom to escort me to the superintendent's office.

I had just finished my first season as a high school basketball coach, and unbeknownst to me, I was being ushered into a meeting with the administration to discuss a litany of parent complaints that arose during the season.

The superintendent had done his homework. He talked with every parent who demanded to be heard. We finished that year 1–18, yet somehow I survived. The pressure campaign continued over the years, including letters to the administration, phone calls lobbying individual school board members, and parents cornering the superintendent at the local gas station. Fortunately, the administration had my back. I would not always be so lucky.

I rarely knew who was saying what, but the lesson was clear . . .

Parents cannot be trusted.

My approach to parents was like that of a defense attorney. I carefully laid out our expectations in a manual that, in some years, approached 40 pages. I wanted policies to be clear to cover my back, but most of all, I wanted parents to stay as far away from the team as possible.

Sound familiar?

Coaching has become more complicated than ever due to the involvement of parents in sports. They demand a seat at the table, often acting as agents, coaches, trainers, and psychologists for their children. They are more financially invested than ever before in their child's development, and often have their own identity wrapped up in the athlete's performance. Coaches from youth leagues to the NBA are wrestling with how to handle their escalating influence.

While many have written about the countless examples of abhorrent parent behavior in the news today, no one has taken the time to examine a way forward that equips coaches to do the unthinkable—to build positive relationships with the sports parent by inviting them into the team experience.

That is, until now.

———————————

For most of my career, I would have described the perfect sports parent as one who followed the advice of Dwayne "The Rock" Johnson:

"Know your role and shut your mouth."

But as I worked to become a more transformational coach, I began to feel a hint of hypocrisy. On the one hand, we told parents our program would be built on love. On the other hand, it was quite clear that it only applied to the coaches and players. We wanted parents to recognize the dynamic culture we were building within the team, yet we did everything possible to keep them from experiencing it for themselves.

Even as my heart toward parents began to change, there was still one major obstacle that took years of trial and error to figure out.

I simply didn't know *what* to do. I didn't know where to turn for advice, examples, or encouragement.

In short, I didn't have access to this book.

What you will find in these pages is a message of hope. It is possible to engage with parents in a positive way that broadens your influence, facilitates better communication, and creates a more meaningful experience for everyone.

However, J.P. doesn't just make a compelling argument for a different approach. He also shows us the way. Each chapter is rich with examples of strategies that have proven effective in the real world. Drawing from experienced coaches at every level, J.P. provides the roadmap I wish I'd had when I started coaching 20 years ago.

Gandhi famously said we must be the change we want to see in the world. The more we invest in building partnerships with parents, the more supportive they will become, and the greater transformation we will be able to bring into this world.

Like it or not, the change starts with us.

Let this book show you the way.

With gratitude,

Nate Sanderson
Co-host of *Coaching Culture Podcast*
Two-time Iowa high school basketball state champions
Head girls basketball coach at Mount Vernon High School

UNLOCKING THE POWER OF PARENTS IN SPORTS

A few days after Christmas in 2016, I hit a new low in my challenges with sports parents. Following a typical morning weekend practice, I was leaving the school parking lot when a parent abruptly sped toward me, swerved in front of my car, and blocked my exit. I felt like I was in a movie scene where the bad guys show up and throw a guy into the back of their van. As I stepped out of my car to confront the father of a player I had been coaching for the past five years, he charged toward me with clenched fists and a face flushed with anger, giving the impression that he was on the verge of throwing a punch. Not sure what was going on, I stood frozen in confusion and fear.

Although the altercation never became physical, in some ways I wish it had so people could have seen the damage it left. The verbal assault was unlike any I had experienced before. He had been triggered because I held his son out of practice that morning for showing up late, a team policy that had been enforced throughout the season. Yet, over the next five minutes, this parent went beyond criticizing my coaching. His comments became deeply personal as he challenged my integrity and sanity.

"I am done with you and your crazy philosophies," he said. "The boys would be better off without you."

The criticism, rage, and anger were scary and deeply hurtful. This wasn't just any parent—it was a father whom I had come to know, like, and respect over the last five years. And now, as my team was in the worst losing stretch I had ever experienced in 30 seasons of coaching, this parent's faith in me had evaporated, even though over the years (and this year in particular) I demonstrated a deep level of care for his son. I was left speechless. What can you say in such a moment?

After he got into his car and drove away in a fury, I didn't drive more than 50 meters before I had my very first panic attack. In recent years, the weight of coaching had started to take its toll, and at this moment it had finally caught up with me. On the *Coaching Culture* podcast, my friend Cody Royle, author of *The Tough Stuff*, aptly describes the weight coaches carry as "the accumulation of stress and anxiety resulting from a deep care for individuals and the profound impact and influence one's role holds over them."[1] The sleepless nights, long hours, and time away from my family started to feel like it wasn't worth it when I had to deal with what felt like a lot of parental bullshit.

I don't give up in life, but that day brought me as close to giving up as ever. I nearly listened to the words of that father and quit mid-season. But I didn't. I persisted. And then six years later, one month after publishing my second book, *The Culture System*,[2] where I recounted the story of that panic attack, I received a random text from that father who still had never apologized for that day. He wrote:

"Hello coach! How's it going? Hopefully all is well. This is Danny's dad. All is well on this end. Danny is doing well. I was having a conversation with friends the other day, a conversation that comes up every so often discussing some of the best coaches that I came across during my son's time being involved in sports. My answer is Coach Nerbun. I often told Danny that with each coach we encounter, at the end of the season, there should be at least one thing we learned and can take with us. Although we learned a lot concerning the game of basketball from you, here is why you are my favorite coach. You were straightforward, fair, firm, and honest with Danny. Hell, you were the same with me. Some of the conversations, whether pleasant or not, made big impacts on how I looked at my approach to raising Danny, which was definitely needed as he came into his later teen and young adult years. So thank you for being Coach Nerbun."

When I got this message I was overcome with emotion. My wife too was moved to tears upon reading it. For coaches, criticism from parents can be deeply hurtful and can impact not only them, but their loved ones as well. The highs and lows of the coaching experience are felt by the family as they are the ones often dealing with the wreckage. In many ways, the father's message helped to not only validate my work in sports over the last five years but heal the wounds inflicted by many parents.

The message taught me a valuable lesson. As coaches we not only have the power to influence the athletes we coach, but also the parents of those athletes. This father credited me with making a big impact on how he raised his son during a critical period in his development. As someone who still remembers being accosted in a school parking lot and told that my coaching philosophies were crazy, this realization was truly mind-blowing.

The message made me wonder how much more of a positive influence I could have had on athletes if I had intentionally leveraged this potential to influence parents. How much more buy-in could I have gotten for the culture I was working to create?

Despite the team's successful turnaround that season and the affirmation I received six years later, I realized that my approach to parents was flawed. Rather than viewing parents as potential partners and allies, I had seen them as a problem to avoid or even remove from the equation. My approach prevented me from fully leveraging the potential influence and impact I could have had on both the athletes and their families. It hindered my effectiveness as a coach, leader, and someone who desired to positively influence the lives of athletes.

Why I Wrote This Book

Every coach experiences challenging moments with parents, whether it's dealing with difficult individuals or even well-intentioned parents who have lost perspective. With over 15 years of coaching, I've quite the collection of moments—from parents coming into the locker room crying after a game about their son's playing time to a parent leaving me a dozen drunk voicemails with incoherent advice. Unlike some coaches I know, I was lucky not to have been physically attacked, had my tires slashed, or endured a parent campaign to get me fired.

A quick search for "sports parents" on Google reveals that I'm not alone in my experiences, with the majority of articles casting them in a negative light. You'll encounter articles like "World Cup scam highlights a big problem: The nightmare sports parent" from the *Washington Post* and "Sports Parents, We Have a Problem" from *Psychology Today*, coupled with advice articles like "Getting Bad Sports Parents to Behave Better."

Difficult sports parents are not confined to particular sports or regions of the country. They are not even confined to parents per se. "Parents" is just the shorthand I'll use when talking about any family member or guardian—grandparent, aunt, or longtime family friend—who is invested in the well-being of an athlete. In fact, coaches at all levels consistently identify parents as the primary issue in today's coaching environment. And while there have always been difficult parents, those of "Generation Z" (born between 1997 and 2012) have earned a reputation for coddling their children and working hard to protect them from any pain or disappointment. As a result, an athlete's lack of toughness, poor attitude, or sense of entitlement can often be directly attributed to their parents. In many cases, parents actively work against the team culture that coaches are trying to build, discrediting their messages and lessons.

Some parents initially appear supportive of coaching goals and standards, only to reveal their true colors when their child fails to receive the playing time they feel entitled to. It's disheartening to witness how quickly they shift their attitude from cooperation to entitlement. Their support appears to be solely contingent on their child's success and their own personal satisfaction. This is a common experience for coaches, and it can be incredibly difficult to navigate. Experiences like these leave coaches distrustful of every parent—even the sane and well-intentioned ones.

It comes as no surprise then that the number one reason why coaches are leaving the profession in droves is due to parents. In a survey from 2017, 82 percent of coaches reported that dealing with parents has gotten worse throughout their coaching careers.[3] This is not just the crazy sports parent captured on camera getting into a fight with the coach, referee, or another parent. Every team has a parent or small group of parents who absorb coaches' energy, keep them up at night, and have some coaches living in fear of losing their jobs. No coach should endure a life filled with fear, abuse, or incessant criticism, particularly considering that more than two-thirds of coaches receive no compensation and engage in coaching primarily to make a positive impact.

Since 2017, I've been writing and podcasting about leadership and culture in sports, and I've received thousands of messages from coaches seeking help with team issues. Without a doubt, even at the collegiate level, parents are the number one most common issue. Throughout my consulting and coaching career, I have witnessed the challenging situations that coaches face, including false accusations, lawsuits, parent uprisings, and even bullying. The pain from these experiences can be traumatic for coaches and their families, creating even more barriers in our already complicated relationships with parents.

I've written this book for the coach who has experienced resistance and criticism from parents but remains committed to coaching and making a positive impact in their athletes' lives. This book is for the coach who wants to cultivate positive and life-changing relationships with their athletes, challenge them, and help them grow. It's for the coach who seeks to create a team culture where players and parents alike are dedicated to the team's success and willing to make personal sacrifices for the greater good. Above all, this book is for coaches who are open to trying a radically new approach and willing to challenge their own thinking, recognizing that there may be better ways to achieve their goals.

I want to be clear: this book is not for coaches who cling to outdated coaching methods and a top-down, authoritarian leadership style. It's not for coaches who blame others for their team's struggles and are unwilling or unaware of the need to make changes in themselves and their approach. This book is for the coaches who are willing to evolve and grow, recognizing that positive change starts with self-reflection and a willingness to try new things.

How This Book Will Help You

In the early stages of his career, Steven Spielberg faced a daunting challenge that could have spelled disaster for the budding filmmaker. While filming the movie *Jaws*, the crew was confronted with a major setback. The mechanical shark, which had consumed a significant portion of their budget, repeatedly malfunctioned, causing extensive delays and rendering entire days of filming useless. The malfunctioning shark not only caused the film to go over budget, but also put it behind schedule.

Spielberg's turning point came when he realized that the defective shark was not the main obstacle. Instead, he recognized that his approach to the problem needed to change, leading him to pivot his thinking and make significant script revisions. This ultimately resulted in a shark movie without an actual shark. This revolutionary approach proved to be a stroke of genius, as *Jaws* went on to shatter box office records, becoming an all-time classic. The film's triumph lay in the power of suggestion, with the absence of the shark creating a profound impact on the audience.

Like Spielberg's faulty mechanical shark, parents are not actually your problem. More likely, the problem is *your approach* to the parents in your program. Rather than providing a solution to your "shark problem," this book provides a new perspective on the challenges of sports parents, suggesting that parents can be valuable partners in your athletes' development and therefore part of the solution. By reshaping your relationship with parents and how you engage with them, you can change the story of your athletes and teams, resulting in more positive and beneficial outcomes.

In most circumstances—despite what we might like to believe—coaches are not the primary influencers in the lives of young athletes. Parents are. Engaging with them in the right way can lead to productive relationships that positively impact the lives of athletes. And that impact isn't limited to the playing field. Richard Weissbourd, professor of moral development at Harvard University and author of *The Parents We Mean to Be*, offers this insight into the outcomes of effective coaching: "Coaches should recognize, too, that while there are advantages to creating a temporary space where children are insulated from family pressures, ultimately their job is not to rescue children from their families but to strengthen the tie between parent and child that is at the backbone of children's healthy development."[4] Good coaching can strengthen families.

In the upcoming pages, you'll discover stories of other leaders and organizations who have successfully engaged parents, including 22-time national championship soccer coach Anson Dorrance, Navy ship captain Mike Abrashoff, and an elementary school in one of the most underserved districts in America. These stories are not just inspiring, but provide practical insights on how to create positive change within the parent culture of your team.

The book's framework follows the one outlined in my previous book, *The Culture System*. Part One starts with our leadership principles and mindset, which are at the core of the system. There I propose a transformational paradigm for coaches to think about the sports parent relationship that not only underpins effective coaching and a positive team culture but creates stronger bonds with parents. Parts Two through Four detail strategies and methods for *establishing, supporting*, and *enforcing* the culture you aim to create. Part Two focuses on building a partnership in the early connection points in the recruiting process, traditional parent meetings, and in those initial conversations with parents. Part Three offers some ideas on how to strengthen the partnership and minimize issues through improved communication practices with parents and strengthening their connection to the team by creating powerful moments. Last, in Part Four we unpack ways to work with your administration to create some boundaries with parents and embrace and grow through conflicts that might occur.

While the framework roughly follows the timeline of the season, the most important aspect is actively embodying this approach toward parents (rather than merely following a set of steps). You will learn a lot of new tools and strategies: take what resonates with you and leave what doesn't. Effective application of this book will come down to finding what works in your context and implementing it in a way that is authentic to you. Doing so systematically helps you to be consistent and will make it seem effortless over time.

No matter what your current relationship with parents may be, implementing a system for working with them can significantly elevate your team's culture. Leveraging the influence of parents not only reduces tangential issues that consume your time and energy, but fosters stronger relationships, creates positive experiences, and profoundly impacts your athletes' lives. By mitigating the interference that parents can create, you strengthen your team's sense of purpose and improve their performance.

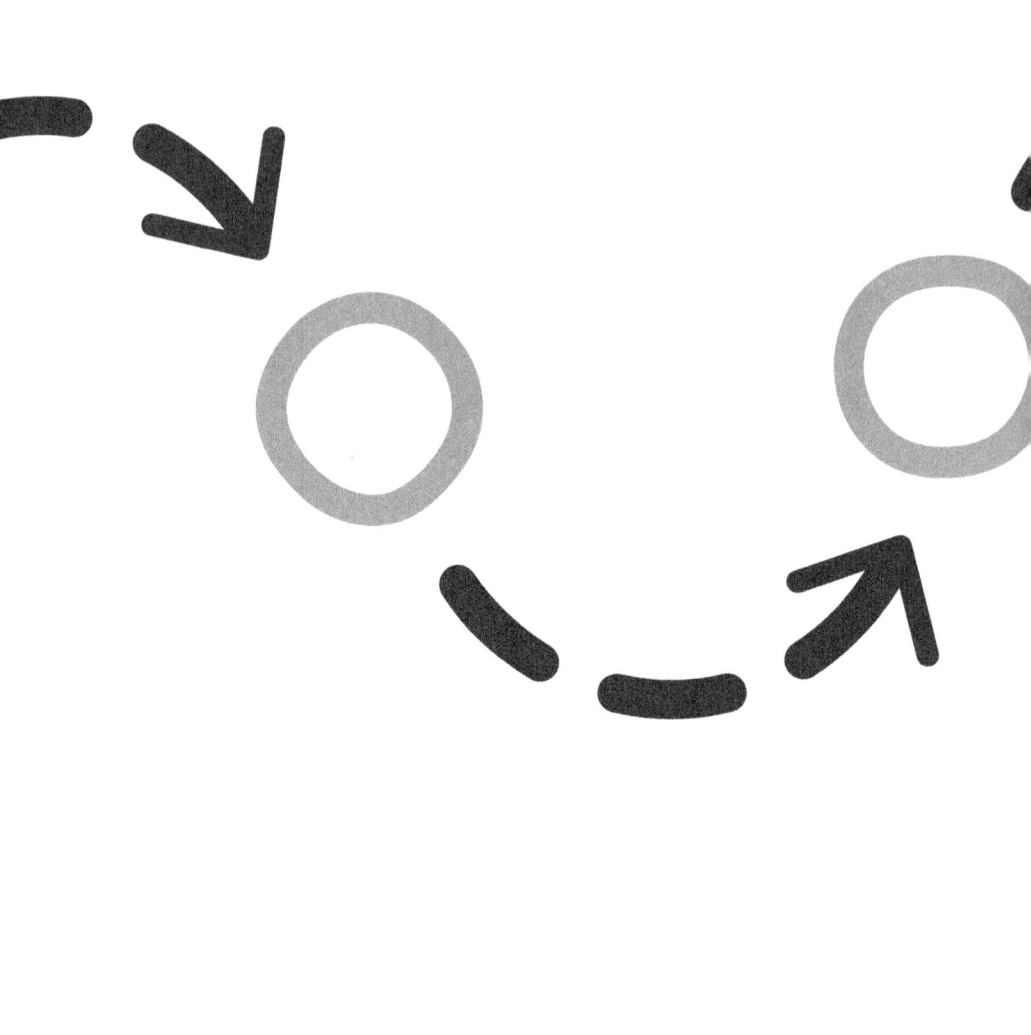

PART ONE
THE CHANGE WITHIN

n Part One of this book, we introduce a radical shift in the dynamics of the sports parent relationship. Chapter 1 takes a deep dive into my personal journey as an athlete and coach, emphasizing the paramount importance of aligning our behaviors with the desired impact we wish to have on the lives of our athletes. Respectful treatment of athletes is a fundamental principle that underpins effective coaching. Throughout this chapter, we will explore core principles that will serve as guideposts on your leadership journey.

In Chapter 2, we explore the transformative journey of a college coach who experienced a breakthrough in his relationship with a challenging player by shifting his perspective on parents. This story serves as a powerful example of how a change in mindset can positively impact team culture. We will delve into strategies that can help you undergo a similar transformation, enabling you to cultivate stronger connections with parents.

No matter where you currently stand on your coaching journey, the change within yourself will be the catalyst for success in your partnership with parents. But it's essential to remember that it's a journey, not an event. By embracing the principles and mindset discussed in Part One, you will become more equipped to create a transformational culture for athletes and their families.

CHAPTER 1

ALIGNING IMPACT WITH INTENT

I grew up playing high school basketball in the early 2000s. The legendary college basketball coach Bobby Knight had just been fired from Indiana University for his old-school coaching methods, which involved emotional (and at times physical) abuse. His dismissal marked a significant turning point in the coaching world, as administrations began to hold coaches accountable for the all-too-common instances of emotional abuse. Unfortunately, for me and my teammates, change came too slowly. My high school basketball coach for four years could best be described as the Bobby Knight of South Carolina.

While it was commonplace to witness coaches yelling and screaming at their athletes from the sidelines, our coach stood out from the rest. He regularly pulled us out of the game, made us stand and look him in the eye, and subjected us to a torrent of criticism for every mistake we made. He would berate us, branding us lazy, selfish, or dumb, only to decide whether to confine us to the end of the bench or thrust us back into the game. The anguish of being humiliated by our coach in front of nearly a thousand spectators still lingers within me to this day. In those moments, I often found myself fighting back tears, struggling to maintain composure amid the overwhelming emotions. Throughout my first three years of playing basketball, I found myself consistently in the crosshairs of his fury.

Parents and fans in the stands remained blissfully unaware of the dark reality that unfolded behind closed doors. The spectators' perception of our coach's behavior was limited to what they witnessed on the sidelines during games. Little did they know that the true magnitude of the emotional abuse was unleashed within the confines of the locker room. It was there that our coach, unrestrained by the presence of outsiders, invaded our personal space and went nose to nose with us. His anger flared and his face grew hot. Saliva gathered at the corners of his mouth, ready to launch onto our faces.

Our coach's wrath was often selective, targeting one or two athletes at a time. Halftime became an agonizing ordeal as he would mercilessly target a single athlete and relentlessly break them down, leaving them emotionally shattered. Emerging from the locker room felt akin to a boxer who had just endured a grueling 15 rounds with the Mike Tyson of emotional battering.

Practices offered no respite from the torment. The piercing sound of his whistle was enough to send chills down my spine. Every pause in the action became an opportunity for him to unleash a torrent of yelling, screaming, and degrading remarks that chipped away at our self-esteem. Over the years, I endured physical aggression as well—jerseys grabbed, arms seized, fingers repeatedly jammed into my sternum. I witnessed a teammate being struck in the head by a kicked ball. We were told that he had to break us down to build us back up, as it would shape us into resilient men. Yet the constant fear, shame, and humiliation took an immeasurable toll on our well-being as young athletes.

Recognizing the detrimental impact the emotional abuse was having on my mental and emotional state, my parents took the proactive step of enrolling me in therapy. Amid the relentless trauma, I found myself teetering on the edge of despair, frequently contemplating suicide. The sport I had once loved had become a source of fear and anguish. Therapy provided me with some tools to cope and survive, offering a lifeline amid the storm. However, the focus was primarily on managing the immediate aftermath of the abuse, rather than delving deep into the healing process and working through the extent of the profound damage he inflicted.

During our time under his coaching, the true extent of our wounds remained largely concealed. It wasn't until years later, long after our time under his influence had concluded, that the weight of the emotional scars began to manifest in painful and profound ways for many of us who had played under him. To this day, these enduring wounds have shaped our self-perception, relationships, and default reactions to stress.

Our Influence as Coaches

My story is just one example of the profound and lasting effects a coach can have on their athletes, whether positive or negative. In our journey of finding solutions for sports parents, we must first acknowledge and take responsibility for our impact. If we don't treat our athletes with respect, no sports parenting solution suggested in this book will succeed. Many coaches mistreat their athletes and then act surprised when parents question their leadership.

In my own experience, some parents, including my own, voiced their concerns directly to my coach and the school administration regarding his approach. However, their voices were disregarded for years. Our coach had enough supporters defending his aggressive style of blaming, shaming, and yelling at athletes that he remained oblivious to the true impact of his actions and failed to take responsibility for his actions. Unfortunately, many coaches claim to have a positive impact on their athletes' lives, yet they hide behind their intentions, refusing to acknowledge the negative impact their behavior has on the athletes. Good intentions do not absolve coaches of harmful actions.

The trouble is that the pain often doesn't stop with the end of the coach-athlete relationship. Unless an intervention occurs, we tend to lead the way we were led and coach the way we were coached. When I began my coaching career, I found myself coaching in the same manner I was coached. I did not know how to correct or discipline differently. While I used my passion and intensity to uplift and inspire my athletes, as the pressures of the job mounted, I gradually succumbed to the familiar patterns of my abusive high school coach. Similar to him, I had enough support from former players, their parents, and stories of positive impact to shield me from any complaints or criticisms for years.

It wasn't until nearly a decade into my coaching career that I recognized the misalignment between my intentions and impact. One pivotal moment occurred midway through the season when a father approached me and requested a conversation in my office after practice. He acknowledged my good intentions as a coach, recognizing my desire to develop the character of the young men on our team. However, he expressed concerns about the impact of my leadership. He raised issues regarding my behavior on the sidelines, the language I used in the locker room, and the lack of discipline within the team.

Deep down, I knew he was right: my actions and the culture I fostered were not having the positive impact I desired.

That's when I discovered a profound source of insight in Joe Ehrmann's book *Inside Out Coaching*. Ehrmann's words resonated deeply within me, encapsulating a profound truth that I had to confront head-on:

> Hurt people hurt people. Wounded boys become wounding men unless there is an intervention, an enlightened witness or mentor-coach to guide them. Wounded adults have to make an honest assessment of their life narratives. If men and women don't transform their pain, they will transfer it to their own children, no matter how much they love them. They will transact with people and athletes to get what they think they need to quiet the voices echoing in their minds.[5]

After multiple interventions, I was ready to accept responsibility for the most crucial change that needed to occur within our team: my own transformation. Motivated to confront my inner demons and break free from destructive cycles, I embarked on a transformative personal journey.

The Journey to Transformational Leadership

The true measure of a leader lies not in relying on ingrained habits and old ways of doing things, but in retraining ourselves and how we operate in the world. The process of becoming a transformational leader extends far beyond simply clarifying "why you coach" and developing a mission statement—it requires a profound journey of self-reflection and personal growth. This kind of inner work includes confronting past experiences that have shaped your identity, conducting a thorough self-assessment of your current state, and understanding the impact you have on the world. Through this introspective process, you can gain clarity on your purpose and direction for the future.

In my own experience, I found various tools to be invaluable in this process, including an intentional reading practice, meditation, journaling, mentorship, and even therapy. Through deep introspection and a resolute commitment to my own development, I was able to break free from the destructive cycle of emotional abuse. This work allowed me to emerge as a coach who embodied more compassion, resilience, and positive leadership and begin my journey of transformational leadership.

In my previous books, *Calling Up: Discovering Your Journey to Transformational Leadership* and *The Culture System: A Proven Process for Creating an Extraordinary Team Culture,* I have provided extensive guidance on facilitating this transformative change. While I won't delve too deeply into it within this book, I do want to share some guiding principles that can assist any coach on their journey to transformational leadership. Although these principles are not exhaustive, they serve as valuable signposts to help you stay on course—and be the kind of coach that you want to be for your athletes and their parents.

Principles for Transformational Leadership

Lead by Example

As renowned UCLA basketball coach John Wooden often said, "The most powerful leadership tool you have is your own personal example." That parent confrontation years ago served as a powerful reminder of this fundamental truth. Despite my dedication to imparting values like hard work, respect, mental toughness, and care for one another through lectures, I failed to grasp that people don't follow what we say—they follow what we do. Our actions and reactions set the tone for those around us, including parents who look to us for guidance and mirror our behavior. This offers a great chance to positively influence parents through our own demeanor, as demonstrated in the introductory story where my compassionate yet firm discipline transformed Danny's father's parenting approach.

When we fall short of being positive examples, we not only undermine our credibility as leaders but also negatively shape the culture among parents. Imagine if every parent behaved like you—what would the parent culture look like? Would there be an abundance of yelling at referees, complaints about players, excuses for losses, or belittling opponents? Our behaviors set the standard for our team. Remember, it's not only the players who observe and emulate us; parents also think, "If the coach is doing it, then I can too." If the only influence you had on parents was your example, what would you do differently?

Own Everything

There's an important truth Coach Dave Brandt, a highly successful soccer coach currently at Bucknell University (and previously at

Messiah College where he won seven national championships), once shared with me about team dynamics and leadership: "If you don't like what's happening on your team, it's your responsibility." This statement highlights the essence of effective leadership. Taking ownership and being accountable for your actions builds trust within the team.

To take ownership, you must admit your mistakes with athletes and parents. Presenting a flawless facade and having all the answers won't foster trust or collaboration. Instead, authenticity and transparency are key. Openly discuss what you are learning. When you freely share challenges and demonstrate personal growth, you foster a culture of continuous improvement.

A great illustration of this in action is Sam Klassen, the head ice hockey coach at Briercrest College. After retiring from professional hockey, he took on his first coaching job at Prairie Hockey Academy in Saskatchewan, Canada. Upon receiving parent feedback forms at the end of the season, he became defensive while reading some of them and felt walls going up. Initially he considered brushing it off and moving forward, but after a call with me, he decided to learn from this feedback. As he humbly shared with me, "I realized the importance of embracing and approaching the feedback with curiosity. Consequently, I reached out to some of the parents who had provided critical feedback and asked them to elaborate and expand on their thoughts. Through this process, I gained valuable insights, which not only helped mend any underlying grievances between myself and the parent, but also deepened my understanding of that parent's connection with their child."

Leaders hold immense power in shaping team dynamics and outcomes. By taking ownership, being accountable, and fostering an environment of trust, leaders pave the way for positive growth.

Be Intentional in Everything You Do

I can recall a moment from my high school days when our coach announced before a game that he wouldn't yell. It seemed like a genuine effort to learn from feedback he had received. However, this commitment to change lasted a mere 20 minutes into the game. At halftime, he burst into the locker room and went off on us. I distinctly remember him saying, "People want me to stop yelling at you boys. I can't. This is who I am."

What prevents someone from becoming a transformational coach? It's not a lack of good intentions; rather, it's the absence of intentionality. Even today, I have no doubt that my high school coach had good intentions. He truly desired to help us become better individuals. The problem lay in his lack of deliberate and purposeful action. He operated on default mode. He was unwilling to put in the work to change. Intentional coaches engage in continuous self-reflection. They actively strive to align their behavior with their purpose. They possess a relentless dedication to finding better methods, abandoning outdated approaches in favor of growth and progress.

Have Conviction in Your Principles

Intentionality involves thoughtful consideration of the right course of action, but conviction takes it a step further by firmly committing to that course of action. This type of leadership requires courage and unwavering belief in our principles, especially when faced with adversity and resistance. As you build relationships with parents, you will realize they have their own barriers and limitations. Even when acting according to your principles, parents may accuse you of having a negative impact on their child. Today's parents often attribute their child's diminished love for the sport or decreased confidence to factors such as perceived unfair playing time or the coach's disciplinary actions. In such instances, remember you are operating based on your principles as a leader, while the parents may be deflecting their child's responsibility for their own experiences, confidence, or behavior. In Part Four, we will delve into effective strategies for responding to these criticisms.

Do the Inner Work

Engaging in inner work is the fundamental starting point for transformational leadership. In order for the strategies, activities, and ideas presented in this book to have a significant impact and lead to success, you must be willing to invest in personal growth. A compelling example of this is Patrick Quirk, the head soccer coach at the Hun School in Princeton, New Jersey. Earlier in his career, when he received an anonymous letter from a parent criticizing his team selection, he reacted by directing his anger and frustration toward the team. He publicly displayed the letter in the locker room, highlighting the critiques, and then made his athletes run the entire practice session.

Since that low point, Patrick has undergone significant changes in his leadership approach and behavior. One of the most remarkable areas of growth lies in his approach to handling parent complaints. Instead of becoming defensive and taking it out on his athletes, he now perceives criticism as a form of care, even when it's difficult to hear. He courageously engages in meetings with parents and their athletes. He actively seeks opportunities to better understand them, build relationships, address any miscommunication, and take responsibility for any mistakes he may have made. As he has transformed, parents have expressed their appreciation for his willingness to listen without defensiveness, explain his thinking while also being receptive to theirs, and follow up on the concerns raised. This is the kind of change we need to witness more frequently among coaches.

Transformational leadership goes beyond mere inspirational statements and a set of core values; it necessitates the visible embodiment of the mission and values in a coach's actions. By choosing ownership rather than defensiveness in the face of criticism, new opportunities for building relationships emerge. While intentionally changing our actions and approaches may be uncomfortable for coaches, it is precisely this intentionality that captures the attention and inspires others through our leadership.

TAKE ACTION

1. Reflect on the following questions:

    ➜ What's the impact previous coaches have had on you, both positively and negatively? How have they influenced your coaching style today?

    ➜ Examine your motivations for coaching and clarify your mission as a coach. What is your purpose and intention behind coaching?

    ➜ Imagine if your example was the only way you communicated with parents. What messages would it convey? Consider the culture that would be created if all parents acted like you. What are some inconsistencies between your behavior and the expectations you have for your players and parents?

2. Be proactive in seeking regular feedback from athletes, parents, and administrators about your leadership and the team's culture. Embrace the feedback you receive to aid in your growth process and take ownership of it.

3. Share the key insights you gain from feedback and commit to making improvements within the team and as a leader.

CHAPTER 2

SEE PARENTS AS PEOPLE

In 2005, Greg Tonagel became the head coach for the men's basketball team at Indiana Wesleyan University. Initially, like most coaches, he perceived parents as a potential problem. But a few years into his tenure, an experience significantly altered his perspective.

Tonagel was grappling with a challenge involving one of his players. A talented rising junior consistently got defensive whenever any coach on staff corrected him. Despite Tonagel's and his staff's persistent efforts to motivate and connect with the player, their attempts always seemed to backfire, as the player remained disengaged and determined to keep emotional walls up. Upon reflection, Tonagel recognized that the player's hesitance to engage with male figures in his life could be attributed to a troubled relationship with his father.

While mowing his lawn one day during the offseason, Tonagel experienced a profound epiphany that completely transformed his mindset. He realized he had seen the father as a problem, blaming him for setting a bad example for his son and sending conflicting messages that went against the team's culture. However, Tonagel now recognized the importance of shifting his perspective and seeing the father as a person.

This paradigm shift opened up a world of new possibilities. He empathized with the father's suffering and distress caused by the strained relationship with his son. Reflecting on his own bond with his children, Tonagel contemplated how he would feel if faced with similar circumstances. He acknowledged that he would welcome any opportunity for support to reestablish connections with his children. Instead of seeing the father as an obstacle, Tonagel now saw him as a human being with his own struggles, hopes, and aspirations for his son's future.

Then Tonagel had the radical idea of inviting all the fathers of the team to attend the summer retreat, which was already a cherished experience for the players. The father-son retreat would offer a chance for them to witness the impact they were making in the lives of their sons through the basketball program. Additionally, the retreat could serve as a way to cultivate stronger relationships and potentially heal the wounds between fathers and sons.

The father-son retreat proved to be transformative not just for the challenging athlete and his father, but also for Tonagel himself. It allowed Tonagel to make headway in his relationship with the athlete, both on and off the court, thanks to the healing that took place between the athlete and his father. The retreat had such a profound impact that to this day the team continues to actively embrace it as a cherished tradition. Tonagel considers it the most significant thing they do within their program, a testament to the power of partnering with fathers and strengthening family relationships.

The retreat revolves around three key elements: adventure, delicious food, and storytelling. Since the inaugural retreat in 2010, the team has engaged in activities like paintball, white water rafting, attending a Chicago Cubs game, hiking, jumping off boulders into lakes, and fishing. However, the most impactful aspect of the retreat is the athletes sharing their personal stories in front of their fathers.

Each year, Tonagel takes the time to express gratitude to the fathers and ask for their support, particularly during moments of adversity during the season. Through the vulnerability of sharing stories from coaches, athletes, and fathers alike, Tonagel creates an environment that encourages openness and connection. He recognizes the importance of fathers in the athletes' lives and seeks to encourage them to be a positive influence.

Instead of trying to be the sole hero of the story and the most important figure in his athletes' lives, Tonagel is reconnecting these young men with the most influential men in their lives: their fathers. These experiences have also forged enduring friendships among the fathers. Tonagel told me one story of a father who shared his personal journey to overcome alcohol addiction. When another father decided to face his own addiction later that season, the first father showed up at his door to offer support.

By involving the fathers in this partnership, the team has achieved success both on and off the court. On the court, they have been one of the most successful NAIA men's basketball teams, winning three national championships in 2014, 2016, and 2018, with a winning percentage of .795. Off the court, the stories of transformation continue to grow, not just for the athletes but for the fathers as well, many of whom describe the bonds formed with their sons as a result of the team as the most significant experiences they have ever had.

Tonagel and his team are committed to a mission of "raising a generation of men who will trade the pursuit of 'me' for the pursuit of three," which is based on their IAM3rd philosophy that puts God first, others second, and self third. By inviting fathers into this mission, they are not only becoming part of the team but also part of the transformation that members experience. As Tim Mangas, the father of one athlete, shared with me, "It's one thing to hear them talk about how they want to help your son become a better man; it's totally different to witness it. Being around the coaches and in that environment changed the way I parented. I used to be the old-school type. The whole experience of being a part of that program changed how I treated my son in and out of basketball. I started to follow Coach Tonagel's example. I was more quick to put my arm around my son and tell him I love him."

Not only do Tonagel's own sons attend, but so does his own father. As Tim explained, "Prior to the retreat I saw [Tonagel] just as a coach, but afterward I saw him as a father and a son." The remarkable results are evident not only in the team's success on the court but also in the continuous development and transformation of both the athletes and their fathers beyond the court.

Outward Mindset: Seeing People as People

The origin of this event and the key to its success is Tonagel's shift from an inward mindset, focused on himself, to an outward mindset, focused on others. This shift—rooted in the principles of transformational leadership covered in Chapter 1—allowed him to see parents as people and welcome their role in helping young men become better people both on and off the court.

When we operate from an inward mindset, we tend to categorize people based on how they impact our own needs, challenges, and desires—as obstacles, vehicles, or simply irrelevant. For example, when we're recruiting talented athletes, we might see with an inward mindset both parents and athletes as mere means to our own success. We might view parents who praise our coaching, support the team at games, and contribute to team functions, fundraisers, or transportation as valuable assets, not individuals themselves.

Let me be clear that it's important and essential to appreciate these positive contributions, but we shouldn't reduce individuals to the roles they play in our coaching journey. That would be objectifying them and limiting our perspective. But what's even more concerning is how this inward mindset often leads us to see parents solely as obstacles the moment they voice complaints, criticisms, or fail to fully embrace our methods. If we truly want to grow as coaches, and help our athletes grow as well, we shouldn't brush off the challenges or issues they raise. Instead, we must genuinely recognize their inherent humanity while approaching matters with an outward mindset.

When we adopt an outward mindset, we start seeing people as individuals with their own unique needs, challenges, and desires, just like ourselves. Parents, in particular, face genuine hardships in life. They deal with job-related stress, financial worries, family illnesses, mental health issues, strained relationships with their children, parenting stresses, and sometimes even connecting their own self-worth to their child's achievements. In the story I shared in the introduction about the confrontational father, I later discovered that he had been going through a challenging divorce.

All parents love their children and want to provide the best for their child. They are usually doing their best with the knowledge and skills they possess. Parenting is widely regarded as one of the most difficult responsibilities one can undertake. It grows more difficult with time, and as children enter adolescence and early adulthood, the universal longing among parents for relationships grows. In fact, Tonagel shared with me that his perspective on sports parents changed forever after becoming a parent himself.

Applying an Outward Mindset

How does one put an outward mindset into practice? Applying this mindset extends beyond individual actions such as arranging father-son or mother-daughter retreats, implementing intentional onboarding programs, organizing team meals with parents, or any of the other activities we will explore throughout this book. Those are all products of an authentically outward mindset rooted in an intentional outlook. The first step is to embody this mindset in every interaction with sports parents, *being intentional in everything you do.* That begins by cultivating three essential qualities: curiosity, authenticity, and gratitude.

Be Curious, Not Judgmental

In coaching, it's common for us to assess parent behaviors in a similar way to how we evaluate players. It's not wrong to want to limit the number of negative parents in our program who are solely focused on their child or likely to cause problems. However, instead of rushing to judgment, we should approach parents with curiosity and work to get to know them as individuals.

Later in this book, I will suggest many ideas that create opportunities to bring that curiosity into the relationship. A simple yet crucial first step is to learn their names. Instead of referring to them as "Jane's dad" or "Billy's mom," make an effort to refer to them by their real name, not their role. Not only does this practice strengthen the relationship, but it also allows us to view them as individuals with their own identities beyond being a parent.

Once you know their names, delve deeper and discover their stories. Where are they from? What do they do for a living? What have their own experiences been like in sports? Aside from work and parenting, what other interests do they have in life? It's important to find common ground and shared interests beyond just their child's athletic journey. Would you want your child's coach to know this about you? Of course—so *lead by example* and do the same.

Understanding their story will provide valuable insights into their hopes and aspirations for their child. By being genuinely curious about parents, taking the time to learn their names and backgrounds, we lay the foundation for a positive and collaborative partnership.

Be Authentic, Not One-Dimensional

In order for parents to see us as people, we must allow ourselves to be seen beyond just our coaching role. Many coaches often feel the need to maintain a constant coach persona around parents or to conform to certain expectations. However, from my studies and experiences working with some of the greatest coaches, I've learned that they all have at least one thing in common: they know who they are as both a coach and a person, and these aspects are intertwined. They don't consciously try to be authentic; it's simply the only way they know how to be—themselves.

When you step into your role as a coach, bring your whole self. Don't be afraid to discuss your family, background, and interests outside of coaching. Share your personal stories, including *owning the challenges and experiences* you've had as a parent. Don't take yourself too seriously. In fact, one of the most effective ways to build a sense of safety and connection in these relationships is by being willing to poke fun at yourself and talk about your own quirks.

Later in the book, we will dive into how to effectively communicate your leadership philosophy to parents. However, you must establish a genuine connection first in order for this partnership to be effective. Parents need to see you as a person, and they won't be able to do that if you hide behind a facade.

Be Grateful, Not Entitled

I've always been impressed by the actions of Greg Popovich, a five-time NBA championship coach, who regularly takes the time to thank his players for the opportunity to coach them. He could easily assume that his players ought to be grateful for the privilege of being coached by him. Instead, he appreciates their uniqueness, the challenges they've overcome, and the sacrifices they've made to reach their current level. This perspective makes him thankful for the privilege of being their coach and for their trust in him.

I understand that the majority of coaches aren't making millions of dollars like Popovich. In fact, many coaches are volunteers or receive minimal compensation that barely covers their expenses. But regardless of the financial situation coaches find themselves in, expressing gratitude toward parents who contribute to the team and show their support is fundamental to the spirit of teamwork. And we should embrace a deeper level of gratitude beyond how they help us—being thankful for the opportunity to coach their children.

Parents invest significant amounts of time, money, and emotional energy in supporting their children's athletic pursuits. Regardless of their other options, they have chosen to place their trust in you as a coach. Letting them know that you don't take this trust for granted and expressing gratitude for the opportunity to coach their child can have a profound impact. As Coach Josh Strasser, a high school football coach in Indiana shared with me, "Parents and athletes quickly recognize the authenticity of a coach, and a simple 'thank you' goes a long way."

Overcoming Painful Parent Experiences

In Chapter 10, I tell the story of how my friend and cohost of the *Coaching Culture* podcast, Nate Sanderson, faced a group of disgruntled parents and was asked to step down as the high school girls basketball coach at Linn-Mar High School in Eastern Iowa. Fortunately, finding another job wouldn't be a challenge for Nate, given his well-respected coaching abilities and his talent in building championship teams and fostering exceptional cultures. However, the trauma caused by that experience with parents became a significant hurdle for him. Only coaches who have gone through a similar ordeal can understand the profound impact it has on one's confidence and ability to trust. Accepting the head girls coach position at Mount Vernon High School a year later meant that Nate would need to overcome the pain and find a way to trust again.

Importantly, Nate stayed true to his beliefs and embodied *having conviction in your principles*. As a result, Nate has consistently demonstrated exceptional skills in implementing the strategies outlined in this book. In fact, he deserves significant credit for introducing, expanding, or improving many of the ideas presented here. However, what's been most impressive is the courage he displayed in overcoming his painful experiences with parents, leaning in, and actively working to build relationships with them. Nate recognizes the vital role parents play in their children's lives, and he works hard to connect with them as individuals beyond their role as parents of the athletes in the program.

Among the various methods he employs to foster these relationships, simple regular conversations with parents have proven to be the most impactful. Engaging in conversations with over 20 athletes' parents may initially seem challenging, but in reality, there are more opportunities available than one might realize. Nate understands that the offseason frequently provides ideal timing for these conversations. Whenever his players participate in other sporting events, he chooses a seat next to the athletes' parents in the bleachers. In these interactions, Nate has found that simply "shooting the breeze" with parents goes a long way in strengthening the coach-parent relationship.

Similar to Nate, if you've coached youth sports, it's probable that you've encountered disappointment and even emotional pain caused by a parent or two. Overcoming these challenging experiences and rebuilding trust can be a difficult journey. The first step toward achieving this with sports parents is acknowledging their humanity and seeing them as people. Embracing this challenging approach will ultimately serve the athletes, the team, and our own selves in the long run.

→ TAKE ACTION

1. Take the initiative and get to know parents by learning their names and stories to find common ground.

2. Show up as your whole self. Share personal stories and even challenges with parents.

3. Take the time to express gratitude by saying simple expressions like "Thank you for allowing me to coach your child."

PART TWO

ESTABLISH THE PARTNERSHIP

n Part Two, we delve into various strategies for creating a strong partnership with parents while establishing shared expectations. While it may not be possible to implement all of these strategies, it is up to you to decide which ones work best in your specific context and to implement them effectively.

Chapter 3 highlights how an ice hockey academy in rural Canada attracts top talent nationwide by emphasizing their mission and prioritizing holistic personal development. The chapter provides guidance for how to share your coaching philosophy and vision for the team, while also gaining a better understanding of parents' needs and beliefs. You will learn how to establish connections among yourself, parents, and athletes, fostering a sense of unity and support.

In Chapter 4 you'll discover how some high school and collegiate coaches are onboarding parents in some radical but exciting ways. You will explore ways to actively involve parents in the team experience, fostering a sense of camaraderie and collaboration. By forging these connections, you not only strengthen your relationship with the parents but also create a supportive network among the athletes and their families.

Chapter 5 recounts the story of a school on the brink of closure that turned everything around by having the courage to visit parents in their own homes. You will learn how to create open lines of communication within your partnership with parents so that they see you as an ally rather than just a coach. You'll gain valuable insights into fostering effective communication channels, including discussions about sensitive topics such as mental health and concerns at home.

While reading through these chapters, you may encounter suggestions that are at odds with your current approach, or you may have concerns about challenging situations such as dealing with difficult sports parents. Remember that Part Two is part of a comprehensive framework, intricately linked with Parts Three and Four, where many of your questions and concerns are likely addressed, providing further guidance and reassurance.

CHAPTER 3

SHARE YOUR COACHING PHILOSOPHY

I t's the month of May, and even with the ground still covered in snow, families gather in the little village of Caronport, nestled in the prairies of Saskatchewan. These families have traveled far—often over a thousand miles—in hopes of securing a spot at Prairie Hockey Academy (PHA), one of Canada's most prestigious hockey academies. Despite its remote location, PHA possesses a unique allure that attracts exceptional talent by offering high school athletes an extraordinary experience. Their mission is crystal clear: to utilize the power of hockey to develop champions in life.

As nearly one hundred athletes and their parents arrive for the showcase, they quickly realize that it's more than just a day filled with drills and games. The experience kicks off with a talk from Justin Simpkins, the founder of PHA, who acknowledges the leadership void within the broader culture. He established PHA with the explicit intention of addressing this void by nurturing the leadership skills of both athletes and coaches. Justin captivates the parents present with powerful stories of previous alumni who were transformed by their experience at PHA, sharing their initial fears of leaving home, the challenges of demanding travel and rigorous academics, and an intense training schedule.

Sharing the mission, vision, values, and high standards of PHA goes beyond Justin's talk. Throughout the weekend, as players compete and are observed, they also take part in character-building exercises in the classroom. PHA doesn't wait until athletes join their academy to initiate the transformation process. They believe that everyone attending their events should have the opportunity to experience personal growth, regardless of whether or not they become part of PHA.

All the athletes participate in a workshop called "Guide to Greatness," where they delve into a variety of thought-provoking questions. These include the following:

➜   What areas of character growth do you need to focus on, and how can you achieve it?

➜   If you were to define yourself in four "I am" statements, what would they be?

➜   What are your top five priorities?

➜   What is your big dream?

➜   What beliefs do you need to let go of in order to move forward and fulfill your true potential?

Under the guidance of coaches, the athletes complete the comprehensive seven-page document that serves as a reflection tool. This exercise, shared with their parents, mirrors the character-building workshops regularly conducted at the academy. PHA understands that merely talking about their mission of developing life champions who strive for excellence is not enough; they are committed to providing an immersive experience that allows athletes and parents to truly embrace this mission.

The spring showcases represent just one example of how PHA seizes every opportunity to share their vision for the organization and their athletes. At any event you attend throughout the year, you'll notice their branding of "developing life champions" on every T-shirt and coffee mug.

Their website, www.prairiehockey.ca, proudly illustrates their extraordinary approach, featuring a home page video that tells the inspiring story behind their foundation. During every recruiting call, coaches take the time to passionately explain to parents why they coach at PHA. By the time athletes and parents arrive on campus for their onboarding week, it's clear to everyone that they are not just entering a high-performance ice hockey academy—they have arrived at a school dedicated to life and leadership.

Sharing your philosophy with athletes and their parents, just like PHA does, is a critical step in establishing a strong foundation and fostering a successful partnership. Finding opportunities to communicate your philosophy—whether it's through an information meeting before tryouts, the first practice, or even a simple email introducing yourself and your approach—is crucial to achieving your goal of transforming your relationship with parents.

Here are several keys to sharing your philosophy clearly and effectively.

Know Your Philosophy

Before you can share your philosophy, you must know your philosophy. While the contents of one's philosophy vary from person to person, in my book *The Culture System*, I delve into its components, which include your mission, vision, values, principles, and standards. Here's a breakdown of what each entails:

- ➜ **Mission statement**: Why do you coach? What is your purpose?
- ➜ **Vision statement:** What is your ultimate aspiration for the team and the athletes?
- ➜ **Core values:** What principles and beliefs matter the most to you as a coach?
- ➜ **Principles:** What are the mantras or sayings that encapsulate your mission and core values?
- ➜ **Standards:** What are the essential behaviors that both you and your players must consistently demonstrate for success?

If you're unsure about your philosophy, I recommend referring to Part One of my book *The Culture System*, which guides you step-by-step in developing and documenting a clear philosophy. You can use this document to continuously reflect on and improve your journey, and you may even consider sharing it with parents and athletes.

Every philosophy has a story behind it. It could stem from your personal history as an athlete or a significant moment in your coaching career. The key is to be able to articulate your philosophy confidently and effortlessly because you'll be discussing it frequently. Collect these stories and share them often, as they can be a powerful means for sharing your philosophy.

Be Direct

Dave Brandt emphasizes the importance of "preparing the soil" when sharing his philosophy. In an interview on my podcast, he shared his approach, saying, "This isn't lip service. It's not what someone is supposed to say in the recruiting process. I will sit them down, open their mouth, shove my philosophy down their throat, then close their mouth, and make them swallow it. This isn't done in a negative way. But I want them to decide, 'Is this good stuff?' And that will make a kid think, so by the time they decide to come play for me, the soil is prepared."

The lesson here is that when communicating your philosophy, be direct. The more direct you are, the less confusion you create. Avoid being overly casual when it's time to share your philosophy about what's important to you, your concerns for today's athletes, and your hopes for their son or daughter. Simply say in your own words, "I'd like to take some time to share a little bit about my coaching philosophy and approach." Then speak with conviction about your beliefs. It's your conviction that inspires, not a fancy slogan or mission statement. The more conviction you speak with, the more parents and athletes will believe in the significance of your philosophy.

Brandt emphasized the need for clarity at Bucknell, where academic standards are high. When parents inquire about the balance between academics, soccer, and social life, Brandt doesn't sugarcoat it. He tells them straightforwardly, "There are two number ones here—academics and soccer—so there is no time for number twos. They won't have much of a social life outside of soccer." This statement carries significant weight, especially at Bucknell, where the fraternity culture is prominent. Unfortunately, many coaches take the opposite approach, enticing players to join their program during recruiting by painting an overly rosy picture. Instead of telling parents and athletes the truth, they focus on why they believe the players will be happy on their team.

In the end, being upfront about your philosophy builds trust and sets clear expectations. By communicating honestly and boldly from the beginning, you create a solid foundation for athletes and parents to make informed decisions and to fully commit to your program.

Find Opportunities for Conversations

While group settings can be the most efficient ways to communicate, it's best to share your philosophy in a personal conversation. Identify the first opportunity to initiate a conversation with the parents of an athlete. This can occur during recruitment, a school tour, a club information meeting, prior to tryouts or the first practice, or even when the athlete chooses to join your team. In addition to giving you the opportunity to share information about yourself, conversations serve as a valuable tool for learning about the athlete and gaining insights into how to effectively work with their parents. Start these conversations by getting to know a little about them and look for some common interests or connections with your own experiences.

Here are some examples of questions to begin early-stage conversations with parents:

1. How did you end up here? What led you to consider our team?
2. Where did you grow up? What was your experience with sports during your childhood?

3. What is most important to your family? What values do you prioritize?

4. What are your greatest concerns for your child? What do you hope they gain from participating in sports?

5. What skills or qualities would you like your child to develop through sports?

6. What goals do you have for your child in sports? What are any broader life goals you hope they achieve?

7. Is there anything important about your son or daughter that we should know but that we may be unaware of?

These conversations also serve the purpose (mentioned in Chapter 1) of getting to know their names and stories—something that's near impossible to do in a meeting.

Share Your Philosophy During a Welcome Meeting

Hosting a preseason meeting for parents, such as an information meeting or a kickoff to the year, provides a fantastic opportunity to share (and reiterate) your coaching philosophy. Sometimes this might be an event only for new parents, but it can be powerful to include returning parents as well. The meeting can serve as a refresher for them and an opportunity to connect new parents with other parents in the program.

Your welcome meeting can include various elements, including discussions about your philosophy around strategy, player development, and even playing time. You will need to decide what works best for you and how you can keep this meeting under an hour. Here are some suggestions for elements you can include in your meeting.

Parent Philosophy

Before delving into your own agenda, create a sense of partnership by inviting parents to share their perspective and concerns. Distribute a questionnaire or notecards to gather valuable insights by asking some of the questions mentioned earlier. This approach proves particularly valuable if you haven't had the opportunity to meet with parents individually or if you want to save certain questions for the meeting. Following Joe Ehrmann's suggestion from his book *Inside Out Coaching*, you might ask parents to list their three to five greatest concerns for their child on the front of the notecard and the three to five reasons they want their child to play sports on the back.[6] During the meeting, you can discuss and outline your coaching strategies for addressing these concerns.

Another effective method to encourage open dialogue is to invite veteran parents to provide advice and share their experiences within the program. For example, I've seen coaches give a few parents who exemplified the desired culture the opportunity to speak up and discuss the challenges they've faced, the valuable lessons they've learned, and the positive influence the program has had on their child.

Coaching Philosophy

When preparing for their presentations, most of the coaches I support include their coaching philosophy in a few slides, along with other relevant information for the meeting. I also highly recommend including a story or two from your own journey as an athlete and coach to provide insight into your "why" as a coach. Sharing a significant moment from your life will help build trust and a stronger connection with the parents.

Culture Philosophy and System

The more transparent you are about your strategies for building the culture and the reasons behind them, the more the parents can get behind them. Consider addressing some of the following areas of concern during the meeting:

→ **How will you establish behavioral standards?** If you have a list of rules, share that with parents. If you take a co-creation approach with the team, explain how it helps build a player-led culture.

→ **How will you build personal relationships with each athlete?** If you have monthly one-on-one meetings with athletes, explain the purpose behind them.

→ **How will you build team cohesion?** If you plan to have occasional team events outside of practices, clarify the purpose behind those activities.

→ **What leadership system will you use?** Whether it's a traditional captain model or a leadership council, share this information now.

→ **How will you challenge athletes and enforce standards?** If you don't resort to yelling and screaming on the sidelines, it may be necessary to explain your approach. Whether you use logical consequences as outlined in *The Culture System* or take a different approach, make sure everyone is clear on what that will look like.

High school girls ice hockey coach Lance Knudson learned a valuable lesson in his first year at Dickinson High School. When the time came to enforce consequences he had previously agreed upon with his athletes, issues arose because the parents had not been properly informed and educated about his nontraditional approach to accountability. When he took the time to explain his philosophy, parents ultimately supported his efforts with their daughters—but not without a lot of recriminations occurring first. If Knudson had taken the time to share his philosophy at the beginning of the season, things would have unfolded much more smoothly, and parents would have been on board from the beginning.

Tactical Philosophy

In any sporting event, it's common for fans to critique and question the decisions made by coaches and players. Like many coaches, you probably find yourself getting defensive whenever a parent asks a question or offers a suggestion. However, it can be valuable to proactively discuss these issues so parents better understand your teaching methods and system of play to avoid potential issues. Explaining the reasoning behind your tactical approach is often interesting to parents as they gain a better understanding of the "why" behind your decisions, which can lead to a greater appreciation for the sport and your coaching methods. Some coaches have found it effective to conduct a comprehensive coaching clinic where they explain their tactical philosophy and answer questions parents may have. For returning parents, you might discuss the tactical changes you are making in the upcoming season in the context of lessons learned from the previous season or changes in personnel. By openly sharing these insights, parents will feel more connected to the team and understand that your decisions are strategic and in the best interest of the team.

Playing Time Philosophy

Playing time is a recurring issue coaches face regardless of the age or level of coaching, and I address this topic throughout the book. As you progress to more competitive levels, share your playing time philosophy in early meetings or conversations, because not every athlete will receive equal playing time. Managing expectations and clearly communicating the reality that playing time will not be evenly distributed among all players is crucial. You can minimize various parent-related issues by transparently sharing how you make playing time decisions, how you communicate these decisions to the athletes, and how you support them.

However you make decisions, helping parents understand the complexity and intentional thinking behind these decisions is important. Acknowledging that you might not always make perfect playing time decisions (no one does!) and assuring the athletes and parents that you actively review such decisions and learn from any mistakes will build even more trust in your playing time decisions.

When communicating playing time decisions to athletes, I strongly discourage the approach I followed for years, which involved simply writing some names on a board a few minutes before the game and expecting players to accept it without question. Based on my personal experience, that approach does not work very well! Instead, consider developing a consistent method for communicating the lineup at the start of the season and any changes throughout. This method should also provide athletes with feedback, support, and occasionally the opportunity for discussion. Whatever method you choose, share it with parents as well, because one of the most common parent complaints is that their child doesn't understand why they aren't playing.

Addressing how you will support their son or daughter in reserve roles is also essential. Since playing time will be limited for reserves, find other ways to demonstrate care and appreciation. Parents want to know that you will continue to invest in their child's growth and development as players, offer opportunities for them to earn more playing time, and reinforce their value as important members of the team.

The Value of Transparency

Brennan Malone, a three-sport coach at Perry Central High School, was determined to establish a clear team standard: "everything matters." He didn't just talk about it with the players and parents, but he also emphasized that there would be consequences for falling short and that privileges would be lost.

When Brennan's star player showed a lack of effort and focus during warm-ups, he made a last-minute lineup change right before the game and openly explained his reasoning. The athlete was furious and displayed terrible body language throughout the game.

The following morning, when Brennan arrived at school, he was surprised to find the athlete and his mother waiting by the front door. Instead of being reprimanded, he was invited into a meeting with the athlete and his mother in the principal's office. To Brennan's astonishment, the mother brought her son to apologize for his lack of effort and assured him that he would do better moving forward.

This incident highlights the immense value of clearly communicating our philosophy. When we are open and honest about our methods, it becomes easier for parents to comprehend and support our challenging decisions. By sharing our coaching philosophy and the specific methods we use to achieve our vision for the team and their child, we not only forge a partnership with parents but also provide them with insights on how they can potentially better parent their own child.

As important as sharing our philosophy is, it's just as important to *consistently implement* our policies and philosophy, as failure to follow through breeds disaster. Even when things go off the rails, by embracing transparency, we empower parents to stand beside us as we navigate the intricate and fulfilling path of coaching, benefiting both the team as a whole and the individual growth of each athlete involved.

TAKE ACTION

1. Get a solid grasp of your coaching philosophy and understand it from the inside out. Be able to communicate your mission, vision, values, and standards with clarity and conviction.

2. Have meaningful individual conversations with parents to share your leadership philosophy and also understand where they're coming from. Consider kicking off the season with a welcome night for parents or offer them some other chance to voice their concerns and for you to share your philosophy.

3. Transparency is the name of the game when it comes to building this partnership. Be upfront and honest about your methods and intentions. The more open you are, the stronger the trust you'll build with parents.

CHAPTER 4

BUILD PARENT CONNECTIONS

Back in 2019, I was working with Coach Darren Douglas, helping him lay the foundation for his new team at Grovetown High School. I went on-site for an exciting three days filled with coach meetings, practice observations, and team-building activities. On the last day, we had a special event planned for the parents—a day we call "the parent experience."

To kick off the day, we gathered in one of the school's classrooms and I led a workshop on healthy sports parenting. I've done this workshop many times before, and it's always a lot of fun. Parents get to open up, have some "aha" moments, and enjoy the chance to discuss matters that too often go unsaid. But on this particular morning, there was one father sitting in the front who seemed resistant to the message. He had a tough demeanor, and it was clear that my message of giving his son space and allowing him to take control of his sports experience wasn't resonating.

After the workshop, we moved to the basketball court, where the players were waiting for their parents. The parents had been told to come dressed for practice because that's exactly what they were going to do. Under the guidance of the team's leadership council, the parents went through an hour-long practice the team designed. They did drills, played games, and even took part in special team traditions like the gratitude circle before practice and celebrations post-practice.

While the parents struggled to keep up with the intensity of the practice, you could see that they were having a blast. There were moments of laughter as mothers and fathers dropped passes, shot airballs, and fell around the court. Toward the end, the players joined in for a few shooting games, and the energy in the gym was upbeat and competitive. As Darren and I watched from the sidelines, we were impressed by how the players stepped up to coach and lead their parents. It was also clear that the parents were impressed at seeing a side of their sons they hadn't seen before.

After the parent practice, everyone sat down, exhausted, and the players served breakfast to their parents. Conversations and laughter filled the gym as parents mingled with each other and with the players. It was far from your typical start-of-the-year parent meeting. As I looked on, I noticed the skeptical father coming up to me. While he seemed to enjoy the practice, I prepared myself for what I thought would be some critical feedback. But he surprised me, saying, "I have to admit, I thought you were crazy bringing us here on a Saturday morning. But I can't remember the last time I had this much fun with my son. Basketball hasn't been enjoyable for our family in a long time. I think you might be onto something—we need to get back to enjoying it as a family."

Over the next three years, Grovetown would rise from obscurity to become the Georgia Class-AAAAAA state champions—the highest division in the state. Coach Darren Douglas credited their success on the court to the work they put in off the court with their culture and developing the character of these young men. And that was only possible because the parents became an integral part of the program. As challenges came up with athletes, he viewed the parents as partners.

After this event Darren found ways to involve parents in almost every team event or trip. The parent experience day has now evolved into what they call Warrior Day, named after Grovetown's mascot. It starts with Darren's yearly parent meeting, followed by the parents participating in practice. They've added more events like an alumni scrimmage, a cookout, and a photo shoot. During the latter, athletes not only get the traditional team and individual photos, but they also include their parents in the pictures. Parents love the opportunity to have a professional photo with their son and his teammates, but it's also a symbol of how they are now part of the team. By involving parents in the team's activities, Grovetown High School built a strong bond between the team, the parents, and the community. It's become a winning formula both on and off the court.

Creating Connection Through the Parent Experience Event

Establishing a strong connection between parents and the team is essential. Parents need opportunities and space to get to know other athletes and parents, build relationships, and bring them together around a common goal. Only when these connections are built are parents able to truly support the entire team and genuinely care for the other athletes.

The aim of this chapter is to present you with ideas for creating your own experience specifically designed for parents. The parent experience can be organized as a stand-alone gathering aimed at cultivating connection, but it is often combined with the parent meeting discussed in Chapter 3. Alternatively, you may choose to run multiple events throughout the year. The format you choose depends on your team's needs and what is realistic for your program.

As the coach, it falls upon you to carefully choose activities that are most suitable for your parent experience event. Connection starts best by having fun together, so I want to begin with some suggestions for time-tested initial activities that have proven to be both popular and enjoyable. These activities can be considered as appetizers for your event, serving as a catalyst for parents to form connections with one another.

Once parents have connected through these enjoyable activities, the foundation will be laid for further strengthening the bonds between athletes and parents—the main course of the event. In a later section of this chapter, I will provide you with effective strategies to accomplish this goal, such as facilitating discussions about healthy sports parenting and establishing behavioral standards for parents that align with the program's overarching goals.

Fun Ways to Build Parent-Team Connections

Team-Building Activities

We've used various team-building activities over the years to help teams build connections, and these activities can work just as well for parents. Two of my favorites are the following:

- ➦ **Spaghetti Tower Marshmallow Challenge:** A team-building activity where participants use spaghetti sticks and marshmallows to construct the tallest freestanding structure within a given time limit.
- ➦ **Speed Dating:** An activity where participants engage in quick, one-on-one conversations using intentional questions. This allows them to meet and interact with multiple people in a short amount of time.

Feel free to adapt any icebreakers you use with your team and incorporate them into the parent experience. Be sure to explain the purpose and message behind each team-building activity.

Parent Practice

Incorporating parents into practices can take various forms. Some coaches choose to design and lead the practice, fostering a dynamic where athletes and parents practice and compete together. On the other hand, there is also the approach of having the athletes design and lead the practice, giving them the opportunity to coach their parents.

A notable example comes from Josh Strasser, football coach at McCutcheon High School, who initiated a unique "Mom Camp." This mini clinic aimed to familiarize mothers with the intricacies of the game, offering insights into sideline conversations, coach-player interactions, and fundamental offensive and defensive concepts. Rather than being mere spectators, mothers actively participated in drills. Nate Sanderson also incorporates a unique activity where he has his athletes draw up a play, attempt to teach it to their parents, and then have them run it during practice. This exercise helps athletes understand the challenges of teaching, while also enlightening parents about the difficulty of remembering plays.

Team Meal

Food provides a wonderful opportunity for people to connect and build relationships. In addition to offering good food, consider being intentional about seating arrangements. I recommend separating parents from each other and ensuring that athletes do not sit with their own parents. This arrangement encourages the formation of new connections and helps minimize the development of cliques even among parents. To make the team meal more seamless for you and more meaningful for the parents, you can assign the athletes the task of serving and cleaning up the food. Some coaches have even gone as far as having the athletes cook the food (although there may be a slight reduction in the quality!). No matter what dimension the act of service from the athletes takes, it is greatly appreciated by parents and is fun for their children.

Team Photos

Offering parents the chance to have a photo with their child in uniform can be a special moment for many families. However, what truly makes a difference is capturing a team photo that includes the parents. This serves as a powerful symbol of togetherness not only for the parents but also for the wider community when shared on your website or social media. Josh Strasser concludes the Mom Camp by having participants don jerseys and capturing the moment in a memorable group photo. If you really want to take it to the next level, consider creating a highlight blooper video of the parent practice!

Meaningful Ways to Deepen Parent-Athlete Connections

Host a Conversation on Healthy Sports Parenting

It can be uncomfortable and ineffective for coaches to lecture parents on how to be good sports parents. That's why coaches have found it beneficial to bring in a speaker like myself. However, you don't need a speaker to create a conversation among parents about what healthy sports parenting entails. This is especially true if the coach is a parent themselves, as it provides an opportunity for parents to share their own challenges.

There are various ways to facilitate this conversation. Sharing a video like "The Truth About Sports Parenting" from ilovetowatchyouplay.com (available on YouTube) can serve as an excellent conversation starter. After watching the video, you can ask people to discuss it in small groups and then share their takeaways with the whole group.

Here are two general discussion questions that I find particularly effective for getting parents to open up:

➡ How has involvement in sports strengthened the bond between you and your child?
➡ How has involvement in sports presented challenges or obstacles in your relationship with your child?

I'll always remember one powerful moment when a father became emotional during a workshop as he shared how he had been treating his son poorly after games, causing his son to refuse to talk to him about football. His vulnerability challenged everyone else in the room to reflect on their own mistakes.

Another successful way I've seen coaches facilitate this conversation with parents is through a book club. While not every parent may join, for those who do it can have a significant impact. My top recommendation for sports parenting books is *What Made Maddy Run* by Kate Fagan, which explores the mental health struggles of a young athlete named Madison Holleran.

However you choose to facilitate the conversation, it's important to be authentic and vulnerable yourself. You don't need to pretend to be an expert on parenting. Consider the case of Jonathan Toczynski, the head basketball coach at Woodbridge High School in Woodbridge, New Jersey. He boldly initiated the healthy sports parenting conversation with parents in his program despite not having any children of his own. The day after the workshop, he received an email from a father who expressed how much Jonathan's presentation on sports parenting resonated with him. The father realized that he had failed to separate his son's self-worth from his performance. He admitted to yelling at him after games and trying to control every aspect of his sporting experience. The father reached out hoping to get more resources to help him become a better sports parent and improve the relationship with his son.

Have Athletes Share Their Team Standards and Expectations

In my book *The Culture System*, I emphasize the importance of coaches and athletes co-creating the standards and policies for the team. This includes establishing agreed-upon consequences and accountability measures. These standards should align with the coach's vision, values, and the team's goals and desired experience for the season. If you already implement this with your team, it can be incredibly powerful to have your leadership group stand before the parents and present the roadmap they have co-created for a successful season.

I also recommend gathering your athletes in a room and encouraging them to co-create a list of three things that parents of the program can do and three things the coaches can do to contribute to the team's success. Encourage the athletes to share these expectations directly with the parents. This activity plays a vital role in empowering athletes to confidently communicate their needs and expectations to both parents and coaches. It can also contribute to my next suggestion: co-creating parent standards.

Create Parent Standards

In his book *Inside Out Coaching*, Joe Ehrmann suggests implementing codes of conduct that athletes, coaches, and parents must sign. While I agree with Ehrmann's recommendation for establishing clear behavioral standards within our program, I have reservations about handing parents a list of rules. Just as I believe we should co-create standards with our athletes, the same goes for parents. By involving them in the process, we are giving them agency over their behavior and impact on the team. This builds greater buy-in—and a deeper connection.

When co-creating parent standards, it's best to keep it simple. Divide parents into groups and ask the following questions:

➤ What should parents avoid doing that could have a negative impact on the team's experience and performance?

➤ What can parents do to help the team be successful and create a positive experience?

After each group has come up with their behavioral dos and don'ts, have them share their ideas. Write all the suggestions on a board and then select the top three to five points that address the most crucial aspects. You can take this final list and share it back with the parents, asking them to sign it or even displaying it as a large poster in the designated "parent section" at games. Parents will struggle to adhere to the standards, but having a reference point can be valuable for addressing any issues that arise later in the year.

Following one of the most challenging seasons with parents in over 30 years of coaching, Andy Cerroni implemented a similar activity with his parents and athletes at Sussex Hamilton High School. By involving the athletes in setting the parent standards, they were able to share how their parents' behavior would impact them. Andy didn't want parents to forget what they had agreed to, so he included the parent standards in the weekly email he sent to parents. Additionally, one parent was given a bag of Tootsie Pops to distribute to other parents before each game. This lighthearted gesture served as a reminder for parents to refrain from making negative remarks or comments below the standards they set when feeling frustrated with officials, athletes, coaches, or the team. It got a lot of laughs and fostered a stronger bond among the parents throughout the season.

Taking the Parent Experience to College

In October 2022, the William & Mary women's lacrosse program in Williamsburg, Virginia, prepared for their highly anticipated parents' weekend. Parents from all over the country traveled to be there for this special event, eager to support their daughters. Head coach Colleen

Dawson, inspired after listening to an episode of the *Coaching Culture* podcast, decided to kick off the weekend with a parent practice. As the hour arrived the weather turned uncooperative as a torrential downpour began. Undeterred, over half of the team's parents braved the rain and joined the practice, which was designed by the players themselves. Some parents had played lacrosse in college, while others were new to the sport. With a contingent of parents cheering on their peers from the sidelines, the playing parents and their daughters slogged through the practice, laughing, competing, and fully immersed in the joy of the moment.

Following the memorable practice, the parents returned to their hotels to freshen up for the evening's main event: the meet and mingle night. This special gathering featured food, raffles, a photo booth, and some of the team's favorite games. The purpose of the event was to foster connections among the parents, ensuring that new families had the opportunity to meet the rest of the team's parents. It also allowed Colleen to express her gratitude to the parents, who played a crucial role in the success of the program. The highlight of the evening was undoubtedly the photo booth, where parents joined together for silly snapshots, creating a bond among the group.

The next day, the parents gathered once again, this time for a tailgate as they cheered on their daughters in a fall ball tournament against other collegiate teams. As the games unfolded, the sense of community and team culture was strengthened. By the end of the weekend, new parents felt welcomed, and returning parents were reminded of the special bond they shared. Every parent recognized their role as not only supporters of their own daughters but also as valued members of the larger program. The unity forged over the weekend would endure, as William & Mary had their best season in recent years. The athletes themselves traced back their success-ful season to the parent kickoff event, with one athlete in particular noting how she had struggled with mental health issues and how the parent experience marked a turning point for her in reigniting her love for the game.

No program is without its struggles, but at William & Mary, the parent culture defied expectations, elevating the athlete experience and positively impacting the team's performance—a rare feat in the realm of Division I athletics.

→ TAKE ACTION

1. Host a parent experience event in your program or include it as part of your official parent meeting. Start by having fun together: do a team-building activity, take team photos together, run a "parent practice," or share a meal. Consider finishing the event by co-creating a set of parent standards for the team to ensure success and a positive experience.

2. Embrace difficult conversations surrounding healthy sports parenting by being authentic and vulnerable. Create a safe space for parents to share their own challenges and concerns.

3. Empower the players to contribute their perspective by sharing their roadmap to success and expressing what they need from the parents.

CHAPTER 5
FOSTER PARENT COMMUNICATION

I n 2010, Stanton Elementary School in Washington, DC, hit rock bottom. It was ranked as the worst elementary school in its district in one of the lowest-performing districts in America. The building was dilapidated, parents were frustrated, teachers were disillusioned, and students were disengaged. In a final effort to turn things around, the district took a bold step, replacing the entire administration team and appointing Carlie John Fisherow as the leader of the transformation.

Fisherow developed a comprehensive plan for change, making the difficult decision to retain only 20 percent of the existing employees after consulting with the previous staff. The school underwent a transformation with new administration and teachers, an updated curriculum, and even a renovated building. However, the situation did not improve and arguably worsened. Unexcused absences and suspension rates soared despite the efforts to turn things around, and teachers felt increasingly disheartened.

Recognizing the disengagement of parents as a result of mistrust in teachers and administration, Susan Stevenson from the Flamboyan Foundation introduced an innovative idea—home visits. Teachers were trained and encouraged to visit parents in pairs, engaging in meaningful conversations within the comfort of their homes. The focus was on building genuine connections and listening to parents' perspectives. Skepticism and fear were initially present as neighborhoods they would visit had a reputation for being dangerous and the concept of home visits seemed like a desperate measure with no guaranteed success. But the approach quickly resonated with both teachers and parents, fostering trust and understanding.

Melissa Bryant, a teacher at Stanton Elementary, initially had her doubts about the effectiveness of home visits. However, she later acknowledged that they served as a pivotal catalyst for turning the school around. Bryant believed that home visits built a solid foundation for relationships and paved the way for forward progress in the classroom.

Nor was Bryant alone; Stanton Elementary teachers soon recognized the importance of establishing strong connections with parents. Home visits provided valuable insights for sharing teaching strategies, but their primary focus was on fostering relationships and open lines of communication. Parents appreciated the personal touch and thoughtful questions posed by teachers, while teachers gained a deeper understanding of their students. An initially skeptical parent Jerome Watkins described the experience as transformative, saying, "Getting to know the teacher on a personal level, understanding their background and educational journey, it was a game changing experience."[7]

Over the years, home visits became not just eagerly anticipated but an expectation for parents, leading to increased parental engagement. Attendance at school events and parent-teacher conferences soared, truancy rates dropped, and academic performance improved significantly.[8] Stanton Elementary's success with home visits mirrored that of other institutions, including the renowned KIPP public charter schools, which have embraced home visits as a foundational element of their educational culture.

Numerous studies have shown the positive impact of home visits on student engagement and academic outcomes. For example, a 2013 study by the Flamboyan Foundation and John Hopkins University revealed a remarkable 24 percent reduction in student absences for those who received home visits.[9]

Open Lines of Communication

Establishing an effective partnership between parents and coaches relies on establishing clear channels of communication and breaking down barriers that hinder the flow of information. Home visits are one of many powerful ways to establish open lines of communication and foster partnerships with parents, ultimately driving the success of your program. Parents may naturally hesitate to reach out due to concerns about bothering the coach or fearing judgment from others for seeking favoritism. However, by fostering open lines of communication with parents, you can proactively address issues and support each other's efforts.

As a coach, you likely have personally experienced instances where parents' actions have caused hurt or frustration, leading you to build emotional walls. When these walls are up, coaches avoid conversations with parents like the plague. It's understandable to feel this way, as coaches shouldn't have to endure mistreatment from irrational sports parents.

While the ideas discussed in the previous chapters contribute to opening lines of communication, this chapter offers additional strategies such as home visits, parent-athlete-coach conferences, and all-parent meetings. Ideas like the home visits may initially seem radical or daunting based on your past experiences. However, rest assured that in Part Four, we will provide methods and strategies for enforcing boundaries and protecting yourself from parents that just don't get it.

That said, by embracing some of the following strategies, we can create an environment that encourages open and honest communication between parents and coaches, and turn parents who might initially be obstacles into advocates for our teams. This not only benefits the athletes' development but also fosters a stronger sense of collaboration and understanding within the entire sports community.

Ask for Parents' Goals and Expectations

One of the significant turning points for teachers at Stanton Elementary occurred when they began inquiring not only about the parents' goals and dreams for their children but also sought to understand their expectations of the teachers. Years ago, Nate Sanderson shifted his mindset from simply dealing with parents to actively working with them. As a result, he started having parents fill out three notecards at the beginning of each annual parent meeting. These notecards aimed to gather specific information, including the following:

- ➜ What's one measurable goal you have for your child?
- ➜ What's one measurable goal you have for the team?
- ➜ What do you want their experience to be like if they *can't* achieve that goal?
- ➜ What do you want your experience to be like as a sports parent?
- ➜ What can you do to help create that experience?
- ➜ What can coaches do to help create that experience?

Here's another variation of these questions that I learned (and modified) from my friend John O'Sullivan, founder of the Changing the Game Project and author of *Every Moment Matters*:

- ➜ List three things your son/daughter already does well as a player.
- ➜ What is your child's role on this team?
- ➜ List three things you would like to see your child improve upon.
- ➜ List three individual goals you have for your son/daughter.
- ➜ List three goals you have for the team this season.
- ➜ List three things your son/daughter needs from me as their coach to be successful this season.

You can collect this information from them through a home visit, notecards at a parent meeting, a Google Form questionnaire, or a personal email. Allowing them to express their hopes, dreams, and expectations is a good starting point. However, the true game changer lies in finding a way to have a conversation with them about the information they have shared, such as in a parent-athlete-coach conference.

The Parent-Athlete-Coach Conference

It's important to have a meeting with each athlete and their parents early in the season. I have witnessed coaches who specifically conduct their parent-athlete-coach conferences at the players' homes for new players joining their program each year. While it may not be feasible for you to conduct home visits, it is worth exploring alternative ways to meet. Some coaches allocate the first 10 practices of the year to meet with two to three parents after each practice. Others adopt a format similar to parent-teacher conferences, a well-established practice in education. They choose an evening to stay late, set aside a block of time, and create a schedule for every athlete and parent to come in for 15 minutes.

The majority of the meeting should be focused on asking questions and actively listening. You can choose to ask some of the questions mentioned earlier or explore the answers they may have provided to questionnaires or during parent meetings. Conversations with parents and athletes are likely to differ, so be sure to explain the purpose of the meeting in your own words. For example, you could say something like this: "I have invited you all here today because I am dedicated to helping your child reach their full potential as an athlete and as a person. Additionally, I want their experience in our program, as well as your experience as a parent, to be exceptional. I know I need your help in this. In our time together, what can we focus on that will make a difference?"

After actively listening to their responses, you may find it appropriate to share any concerns you have for their child or discuss the role you and the coaching staff envision for them in the upcoming season (further details on this topic can be found in Part Three).

Create an Open-Door Policy

In November 2022, Tyler Wright, the girls basketball coach at Mount Zion High School, received a call from the mother of twin athletes on his team. Tragically, the girls' father had passed away, and the mother was unsure of how to break the news to them or how they would cope with it. Upon hearing this, Tyler cried and prayed with the mother over the phone before springing into action to support the family. Throughout the season, he stood by these young women, walking with them through the grieving process of losing their father.

What made this story so impactful was the fact that the mother chose to call their basketball coach as the first point of contact. Over the years, Tyler had experienced both highs and lows with the twin girls. Through it all he consistently maintained not only a working relationship with them but also kept in constant communication with their mother. Even during the offseason, Tyler would reach out to the mother with a text or phone calls to check in on the family. Their conversations often revolved around the well-being of the twins, discussing how they were doing and whether they were facing any challenges in basketball or life. It was through this strong bond and connection with the family that Tyler was able to provide support during their most challenging times. While not every athlete and their family will experience such tragedies during their time in your program, you should strive to be a source of support for all your athletes and their families in the face of any adversity. By creating open lines of communication, you make that support possible.

In most teams, coaches tend to communicate the conversations they don't want to have with parents. However, I recommend starting by communicating the conversations you do want to have moving forward. Here is my list of the five conversations I want to have with parents:

1. *You don't understand why your child is not playing*: The key here is "understanding." I am fine with you not agreeing with me, but it's important that everyone in the program—coaches, players, and parents—clearly understands how I determine playing time.

2. *When your child is struggling*: You have a unique insight into the emotional and mental challenges your child may be facing, which nobody else on the team sees. Letting me know about any observations—both negative or positive—can be incredibly helpful in coaching the individual.

3. *When something is happening at home:* Home life can present significant challenges. My players have experienced a wide range of difficulties in the past, such as divorce, family member incarceration, terminal illness, or financial struggles. These challenges can weigh heavily on a person. While I don't need to know every detail, I do want to be aware of the family challenges so that I can provide support and compassion.

4. *When you have a serious issue with my behavior*: We all make mistakes. I don't expect to be called out on every single one, but if there is consistent or significant enough concern that your opinion of me as a person has changed, I want to know about it. It's important to me that what I value is evident not just through my words at the beginning of the season, but also through my actions throughout.

5. *When something has been bothering you for an extended period of time*: We all have moments that frustrate us, and

sometimes we need time and space to regain perspective. However, if something has been bothering you for an extended period and I may be able to help you gain clarity and alleviate that frustration, I want to have a conversation.

Many coaches would look at this list of conversations and worry that it might invite trouble, but let me reassure you. Coaches I've worked with who have shared their list of conversations have typically found that having an open-door policy actually leads to fewer parent meetings. The reality is we are going to hear from the irrational sports parent whether we invite these conversations or not. What we can do is counterbalance those interactions with a wealth of meaningful parent discussions.

Establish Boundaries

While opening lines of communication is important, it is equally important to establish boundaries. Failing to set them can result in valuable time being lost that should be dedicated to practicing, planning, grading papers, taking care of yourself, or spending time with family. Instead of being available at all hours, consider setting specific office hours during which they can reach out to you about nonemergency matters.

I personally avoid absolute statements such as "I will never discuss playing time" or "I will not discuss strategy." Sometimes, I find it can be beneficial to share my perspective on these topics. Still, the 24-hour policy is a common practice adopted at many levels, where parents are asked to wait for 24 hours before discussing certain issues. I suggest framing this policy as important not only for the parents but also for yourself. Former Trinity Western ice hockey coach Barret Kropf shared an incident with me where a parent confronted him in the lobby about their son's playing time during the national championship. The team had just lost a close game, and instead of walking away, the confrontation escalated to a point where Barret found himself nose to nose with the parent in front of many others. While the parent's behavior was out of line, Barret acknowledges that he also crossed a line and regrets the example he set in that moment. The lesson here is that the 24-hour policy isn't just for the parents; it applies to us as well. It allows us time to cool down, reflect, and respond in a more constructive manner.

Partnering with Parents to Address Mental Health

While serving as the head swimming coach of Dixie State, Coach Tamber McCallister had a good understanding of her players and the team. However, she realized that some players were slipping through the cracks when a parent unexpectedly flew in for a swim meet. The father approached her and shared that his daughter was struggling with mental health issues. This experience made Tamber realize that it would be impossible for her to personally keep track of all 34 women on her team, and she recognized that establishing a closer partnership with parents was the solution.

The following year, Tamber implemented a new approach. She included parents in the onboarding of each athlete and started instituting a parent-athlete-coach conference. During these meetings, she set boundaries regarding the athletes' responsibility for their playing time. However, the primary focus of the conversation was to encourage open communication with parents, particularly regarding mental health. Tamber expressed particular concern for freshmen who were still adjusting to college life and made it clear that both the athletes and parents could approach her anytime if they were facing any difficulties. Additionally, she took the time to listen to parents and understand any concerns they had about their daughters heading off to college. This tradition has now been brought to Brigham Young University, where Tamber serves as an assistant coach. It is a simple yet effective way to establish a partnership from day one.

TAKE ACTION

1. Organize parent-athlete-coach conferences where you can discuss their aspirations, concerns for their child, and their expectations of you as a coach. Consider conducting home visits for each athlete in your program, whether it's during the recruitment process or for new players joining the team each season.

2. Utilize the six questions by Nate Sanderson or John O'Sullivan to gain insight into the parent's perspective before the parent-athlete-coach conference.

3. Establish healthy boundaries for communication, such as designated times or specific topics that are open for discussion.

PART THREE

SUPPORTING THE PARTNERSHIP

I n Part Three, we explore a range of effective strategies to support and strengthen the partnership between coaches and parents. These relationships require continuous nurturing and engagement.

Chapter 6 presents a story of how an elementary school administrator led a transformative cultural change by implementing a system of consistent communication between parents, students, and teachers. This chapter offers valuable guidance for developing your own communication system, which not only minimizes potential issues but also keeps parents actively engaged in the program.

In Chapter 7 you'll learn from the practices of arguably the most successful Division I coach of all time, who actively embraces and encourages parent involvement within the team. Building on strategies from Chapter 4, you will discover additional ways to include parents in the team experience, further strengthening the sense of community and mutual support.

Chapter 8 shares the inspiring story of Greg Tonagel, who created unique moments that leveraged relationships with parents to elevate his team's performance at the national tournament. By crafting powerful moments, you can instill a sense of pride in parents for their sons and daughters while strengthening their bond with their child.

It is not practical (nor would it be advisable) to attempt to implement every strategy within these chapters. Some of these strategies may already be in practice, but you will discover opportunities to improve and make small adjustments. Other strategies may inspire your creativity, leading you to develop your own innovative approaches to enhance the relationships with parents.

CHAPTER 6

COMMUNICATE CONSISTENTLY

The education system took a hard hit from the COVID-19 pandemic, with consequences that extended far beyond a drop in academic performance. When schools returned to in-person instruction, teachers saw a rise in absenteeism, mental health issues, and increased violence. One issue that ran deep was the breakdown in trust between parents and schools. An article in the *Washington Post*, titled "Public Education Is Facing a Crisis of Epic Proportions," summarized the situation, stating that "parents were screaming at school boards."[10]

In 2021, when Phil Mansueto became the dean of students at Ivy Academy in Chattanooga, Tennessee, he recognized the importance of leveraging his 17 years of experience as a special education teacher by working closely with parents. Responsible for over 300 students, Phil knew that parental collaboration was critical.

To foster communication, Phil started sending biweekly emails to parents, outlining the skills all teachers would focus on in the upcoming weeks, such as teamwork, receiving feedback, and empathy. These skills were not only taught but also reinforced through positive referrals. Whenever a student demonstrated these skills, the teacher would write them up, and both the student and teacher would enter a drawing for a free lunch. Then Phil would personally call the parent to share the good news. As he explained, "I cannot communicate with empathy and compassion in an email. They need to hear my voice and know I am a parent as well. Positive or negative feedback won't be processed the same way if it's lost in their email inbox."

In instances of disciplinary issues, parents were promptly involved. Phil made it a priority to keep them informed about the situation, even calling them on speakerphone if they couldn't attend in person. This approach allowed for immediate parent engagement and understanding.

Since assuming his role, half of Phil's days have been primarily dedicated to communication, with over 1,000 contacts made with parents in 2022. Remarkably, more than a third of these interactions were positive. His goal is to discover and share the good while addressing the negative. Positive and negative consequences are both utilized to reinforce behavior within the school, with a commitment to always inform parents.

The impact of this approach on the school has been significant. There has been a remarkable decline in both in-school and out-of-school suspensions, as restorative discipline practices have taken precedence over punitive measures. Instead of sending a disrespectful student to detention, they now spend time after school assisting the teacher. When a student throws food in the cafeteria, they are assigned to help the cleaning staff with cafeteria cleanup. In cases where two students engage in a fight, they are encouraged to have lunch together, creating an opportunity to understand each other better.

The school culture has also experienced a positive shift, felt by teachers and students alike as they traverse the halls. Parent engagement has reached an all-time high, with increased participation in the school's parent teacher organization (PTO), reflecting the rebuilt trust between parents and the school.

For Phil, the most meaningful change lies in how parents respond to his calls. With not every call being negative, parents are no longer instantly triggered and defensive when receiving a call from the dean of students. Parents are now more willing to engage and collaborate with Phil to support their child's growth. They understand and support the accountability measures implemented, no longer seeking to shield their child from the consequences of their actions.

Phil understands this shift firsthand, being a parent himself. He recognizes that when you aren't aware of all the efforts teachers are making for your child, defensiveness can arise. However, by openly sharing the school's initiatives to support children, he knows that as a parent himself, he is more likely to transition from a defensive to an offensive stance—wanting to actively support the school's efforts.

The Value of Consistent Communication

It's not enough to simply open the lines of communication; we must actually use those lines to *communicate consistently*. Most of us tend to believe we do a good job at communication. Yet organizational research consistently reveals a stark truth: leaders overestimate their communication abilities. Having conducted hundreds of surveys over five years, collecting feedback from athletes and parents, I can confidently affirm that the primary complaint is a coach's lack of communication. Surprisingly, coaches often find themselves taken aback by this feedback, convinced they have gone above and beyond in their efforts. However, as the playwright and critic George Bernard Shaw once declared, "The single biggest problem in communication is the illusion that it has taken place."

During my early work with coaches, we meet to review a 360 assessment, a common performance evaluation tool that gathers feedback from a variety of sources. As one coach and I reviewed feedback from parents, the coach shared with me, "I feel like I've held multiple meetings with parents over the years, and yet their biggest complaint remains my lack of communication." Notably, the coach mentioned meetings with parents, but it's important to recognize that people desire various forms of communication. Far too often we only communicate when issues arise. That's undoubtedly important, but consistently reaching out to parents to share all types of information keeps them informed and makes them feel engaged in a partnership. Consistent communication in a variety of ways is a vital cornerstone of any successful partnership, and the following approaches can help you achieve it.

The Weekly Parent Email

Coaches often engage with parents throughout the year, whether it's through group chats, emails, or communication apps like TeamSnap. They discuss logistics such as practice and game times, fundraising, and team events. Failing to communicate logistics is an obvious frustration for parents as they are juggling the schedules of multiple family members and making sacrifices to support the program. But just communicating the logistics is a missed opportunity to reinforce the team's culture and nurture the partnership with parents.

To improve the chances of parents actually reading your emails, make them interesting. Start by being yourself. The most effective emails to parents are the ones that radiate the coach's passion, energy, care, and enthusiasm. You don't have to be a brilliant writer—just be genuine and put your passion into crafting the email. Initially it may seem like an additional task, but over time many coaches have discovered it to be one of the most valuable ways to prepare for the upcoming week. Composing the email prompts both reflection and proactive planning. Here are six elements to consider including in your weekly email or message to parents.

Reflect on the Past Week and the Upcoming Week

Every fan, whether after a victory or defeat, has a story to share about their team and the latest game. Use the email to frame the narrative in a positive and constructive way for parents. Maybe you played somebody with a losing record, but they just brought back a key player from injury. Maybe you are on a losing streak, but you knew this would be a tough stretch for the team that could help them get ready for the postseason. Whether you had a big win or a tough loss, you want to emphasize what your team is doing to learn from the past and focus on the controllables.

In addition to a recap of the previous week, many of the coaches I support have found it beneficial to provide a brief scouting report on the teams they will be facing in the upcoming week. Parents appreciate reading about the upcoming games, and it helps the coach establish realistic expectations for challenging opponents and a focus for the team.

What We're Working On

Just as Phil Mansueto at Ivy Academy regularly communicates the character skills they teach, train, and reinforce every two weeks, we should keep parents informed about our ongoing focus. While this includes our technical and tactical focus in practices, hopefully we have something more to share than what we are teaching them in our sport.

Following the lead of Nate Sanderson, many coaches have embraced the practice of a weekly mental health or culture day. These sessions often encompass a broad range of topics, such as positive self-talk; skills of great teammates; education on health, nutrition, and sleep; and incorporating mindfulness practices. Regardless of how you prioritize the character and personal development of your athletes, the weekly email presents an excellent opportunity to share the work we are doing with their child.

Celebration and Recognition

It's important to celebrate the team's achievements and recognize moments or behaviors that reinforce the culture. Take a moment to acknowledge what the team has accomplished during the week: perhaps they volunteered in the community, assisted a teacher at school, or displayed a positive attitude even after a defeat.

Resources for Sports Parents

Offering valuable resources for sports parents can be done in a way that parents genuinely appreciate and find beneficial. While it's important not to give direct parenting advice, sharing helpful resources can foster a positive and non-defensive response. Websites such as ilovetowatchyouplay.com by my friend Asia Mape, changingthegameproject.com by John O'Sullivan, or GrowingLeaders.com by Tim Elmore provide insightful blogs and videos with valuable advice and tips for today's parents, coaches, and teachers. Aim to share something each week, rather than using parenting resources as a means to passively address issues that come up.

Thank Yous

Expressing gratitude is crucial, as parents play a vital role in supporting the team through various tasks such as team meals, transportation, and unwavering encouragement. Dedicate a moment to sincerely thank not only all the parents for their unwavering support, but also to acknowledge and appreciate the individuals who made your week as a coach more manageable and contributed to the team's success.

Message from a Captain

Athletes have plenty of opportunities to share their thoughts through social media, but rarely do we work with them to develop these communication skills. Consider empowering your captains with the opportunity to include a short message each week in the email to thank parents for their support and share what the team is working on that week.

Parent Check-In

In my previous book *The Culture System*, I recounted the story of Captain Mike Abrashoff, who transformed the USS Benfold from the worst ship to the best ship in the US Navy within two years. A pivotal aspect of this transformation was Abrashoff's ability to forge connections with all 312 sailors on board. His care and concern extended not only to the sailors themselves but also encompassed their parents, as he took the time to empathize with the sailors from their parents' perspective. Whenever a new sailor joined the ship, Abrashoff personally greeted them and then accompanied them to the bridge to make a call to their parents, assuring them of their safe arrival. In a time before everyone had a cell phone, this small gesture carried immense significance.

During my conversation with Abrashoff, another practice of his struck me profoundly: his habit of writing letters to parents of sailors nearly every day. Recognizing that many of these young men and women had overcome challenging childhoods to join the Navy, Abrashoff placed himself in the parents' shoes. He imagined the emotions they would experience upon receiving a letter from their child's commanding officer. Consequently, whenever a sailor accomplished something noteworthy, Abrashoff would write a letter to their parents. The parents would share their pride with their sons or daughters, and the sailors would be grateful for Abrashoff, knowing he truly cared about each of them.

A few weeks after Abrashoff had sent a letter to one sailor's father, the sailor came to Abrashoff's cabin and had tears streaming down his face. When Abrashoff asked what was wrong, he said, "I just got a call from my father, who all my life told me I'm a failure. This time, he said he'd just read your letter, and he wanted to congratulate me and say how proud he was of me. It's the first time in my entire life he's actually encouraged me. Captain, I can't thank you enough."

While sending positive notes to parents is a commendable action for any coach or leader, what truly impresses me about this story is Abrashoff's mindset. He consistently considered the parents' perspective, understanding the challenges and anxieties they faced with their children far away from home. This unwavering concern for the parents translated into consistent communication from Abrashoff.

Engaging in parent check-ins can make a significant impact. In my own experience as a father, it is incredibly gratifying when teachers or coaches express their genuine enjoyment of working with our children. As parents, we often question our parenting abilities, and receiving these messages not only affirms our kids but also provides validation for our efforts.

During these check-ins, what should we convey? Sometimes a simple expression of gratitude suffices, such as saying, "Thank you for allowing me to coach your daughter. She is an exceptional teammate and brings joy to our coaching sessions." Other times, it may involve offering specific appreciation for something they have done, like "I wanted to inform you that she has truly emerged as a leader for our team. It has been inspiring to witness her work ethic and how she sets the tone during our practices." Other times it could just be sharing what you enjoy about coaching their child.

Not every interaction will be exclusively positive, and acknowledging a struggle is equally important. For instance, reaching out and saying, "I wanted to inform you that I recently spoke with your daughter about her role. She has been feeling frustrated due to her reduced playing time. I provided guidance on areas she can focus on, and I also asked her how we can support her during this challenging period. She expressed that weekly check-ins with a coach would be helpful, so we will continue to stay connected."

It may seem daunting to find the time for these check-ins with parents, but I have witnessed coaches develop a habit of making phone calls a few times a week during their commute or sending personal messages after monthly player development meetings. One coach I supported initially hesitated to prioritize check-ins with players' parents. However, halfway through the season, a parent took to social media to vent their frustration, claiming that the coach did not care about all the players and their child was not receiving the playing time they deserved. In response, the coach began conducting check-ins and sharing updates after every player development meeting. The impact was remarkable and immediate, with the complaining mother soon expressing her astonishment to the coach: "I had no idea about all the things you were doing for my son."

Communicate Conflict

When confronted with conflict, determining when to involve parents and when to handle it solely between the coach and the athlete or team can be challenging. One simple guideline I recommend following is that if the parents will be aware of the consequences, it is valuable to include them in communication about the situation.

I recall an incident years ago when I faced significant challenges with one of my star athletes. His playing time had been reduced due to his lack of effort and negative attitude during practices. Eventually, things reached a breaking point, and I decided to remove him from the lineup entirely. To make matters worse, I informed the player that he wouldn't be playing just one hour before the game. However, I failed to communicate any of this to his mother, which meant she only "heard" the story from her son's perspective as he sulked on the sidelines (which from her perspective was entirely justified as she didn't know why he suddenly wasn't playing). As I headed toward the locker room, the mother confronted me and gave me an earful. Resolving the issue required a substantial amount of my time and energy over the following days.

In situations where discipline is necessary and you wish to maintain trust with the player, simply inform them that you will be communicating the matter to their parents. Emphasize to the parents that your intention is to work together to provide support for the athlete.

Melissa James, girls volleyball coach at Perry Central High School in Indiana, learned the benefits of this approach firsthand. When she became aware of a parent's concern regarding a personality conflict between her child and another player on the team, Melissa arranged a meeting with the mother after the next practice. This meeting allowed Melissa to gain valuable insights about the athlete and better assist the athletes involved in resolving their conflict. The parent expressed immense gratitude for Melissa's proactive outreach and recognized the time and effort she invested in creating a positive experience for the athletes.

TAKE ACTION

1. Enhance your weekly email communication with parents by incorporating the following elements:
   - Share your reflections on the past week's games and events.
   - Provide insights into what you're currently focusing on in and out of practice.
   - Celebrate noteworthy achievements and recognize individual contributions.
   - Share valuable resources for sports parents.
   - Express gratitude and extend thanks to everyone who contributed the past week.
   - Empower your captain to share their thoughts and perspective.
2. Regularly check in with parents throughout the year, whether it's by following a checklist or simply making it a habit to follow up with parents after one-on-one sessions with athletes.
3. When faced with conflicts arising from player misbehavior or interpersonal issues within the team, proactively communicate with parents to address the situation.

CHAPTER 7

INCLUDE PARENTS IN TEAM EXPERIENCES

Anson Dorrance holds the record for the most titles won by a Division I coach with a single team. His incredible journey started in 1982 when his Tar Heels secured the very first Division I women's soccer championship. From 1982 to 2012, the University of North Carolina clinched an astonishing 21 national championships, never going more than two years without claiming a title.

You'd think with such success, Dorrance wouldn't have any parent issues. But truth be told, he has plenty of stories about unhappy parents, including one who confronted him outside his office complaining about his daughter's playing time—the day after winning the national championship!

Nevertheless, for every angry parent, Dorrance acknowledges ten others who are grateful for the positive impact he has had on their daughters' lives. As he once shared with me, he embraces the challenge: "We don't want to hold parents at arm's length because, the way we look at it, the reason their daughters' are so good is the parents. They've invested in their game. To some extent, I owe the parents. Also, I want them to be partners with me in shaping the athletes positively." This perspective has greatly influenced his approach toward parents in the program. While he does small things like openly sharing practice data and being available for discussions regarding parental concerns, his main focus is on ensuring that parents feel valued and included in the program.

Throughout the years, Dorrance has made efforts to involve parents as much as possible in the team experience. He treats every weekend as a "parents' weekend." Parents are invited to attend pregame meetings and join the team for meals on road trips. Those who manage to attend all the games are encouraged to act as surrogate parents for other athletes. Unlike earlier in his career, Dorrance now prioritizes finding a few minutes of playing time for a reserve player whose parents have shown up for a particular game. This inclusive approach strengthens the bond between parents and the team, fostering a supportive and united environment.

Create Opportunities for a Shared Experience

The leaders I've observed who build effective partnerships with parents take a similar approach as Dorrance. They don't shy away from finding ways to include parents in team experiences. For instance, Greg Tonagel extended an invitation to fathers for a memorable father-son retreat, while Phil Mansueto organized a monthly "Parents to Pride Rock," a spirited 5-mile hike on Saturday mornings at Ivy Academy.

Think about it: if parents go the extra mile, driving for hours, staying in hotels, and braving the cold on the sidelines, why wouldn't you want to include them? It's disheartening to witness the growing trend in sports where parents are isolated, not sitting together, and often more focused on cheering solely for their child rather than the team. But here's the thing—it's hard to truly care about a team when you're held at arm's length. While it's not necessary to involve parents in every aspect of the team, it's important to actively seek opportunities to share the team experience with them. Here are some simple ways for you to involve parents in the team experience.

Team Meals

Creating opportunities for parents to share a meal with the team and fellow parents, whether before or after a game, can help foster strong connections. Sussex Hamilton High School basketball coach Andy Cerroni did this by establishing a tradition of coaches and parents gathering at a local restaurant after games. In my own experience as a high school athlete, one of my favorite traditions was how a family would host a potluck for the team and parents after Friday night games, allowing us to celebrate victories and support each other after losses.

Watching Practice

While fictional, the show *Ted Lasso* has provided some valuable coaching insights through the character of Coach Lasso. One moment in particular that stood out to me was when he started inviting fans and family to watch every practice, fostering a stronger sense of community and support for the team.

As a young coach, I initially resisted the idea of parents watching practice, fearing potential distractions. Truthfully, I recognize now that many of my previous concerns stemmed from my own embarrassment about certain things that went on in our practices. However, I later realized some of the benefits of allowing parents to observe from the stands. It provided them with valuable insight into our cultural and strategic approach. Additionally, I came to realize that parents would be present on game days, and athletes needed to learn to focus and block out potential distractions—including the presence of their parents.

Rather than having parents wait idly for their child's practice to conclude, consider extending an invitation for them to occasionally join in. I've personally appreciated how my children's youth coaches would occasionally ask parents to assist with drills or participate in games alongside our kids. They have even shared some fun games that we can play with our children at home. If you coach at the collegiate level and parents are visiting town, invite them to observe practices.

Pregame Meeting

Similar to Anson Dorrance, Indiana Wesleyan University basketball coach Greg Tonagel extends an invitation to parents to join film sessions of opponents the night before a game. This allows parents to witness the scouting and preparation efforts put in by the coaching staff. When parents see the level of detail and planning that goes into the team's game strategy, they are often blown away and gain a deeper appreciation for the coach's expertise.

Even at the youth level, coaches like John O'Sullivan involve parents in the last practice before a game. During this session, parents join the team for a meeting where the week's practice focus and game plan are reviewed. This approach helps parents understand what the team has been working on and what they should be cheering for during the game.

Postgame Talk

Bill Beswick is a renowned sports psychologist with an impressive resume. He has worked with athletes like David Beckham and prestigious teams like Manchester United and the English international football team. However, one year Beswick found himself in a different coaching role. He took on the challenge of coaching a local under 8s rugby team. The team struggled, losing game after game. But Beswick made the decision to involve the parents in the postgame discussions where he addressed the team. His intention was to highlight the positive aspects and ensure that the boys continued to enjoy and learn from the experience, even in the face of defeat. Despite not winning a single game that season, every child returned the following year, and many went on to have successful careers in rugby.

When Andy Cerroni's team won the conference championship in 2023, it was a profound and memorable experience. He decided to share that moment with the parents who had supported the young men throughout their careers, inviting them back for the locker room celebration and postgame speeches. Months later one father shared with Andy, "It was a truly unforgettable moment for me as a proud parent and supporter of the program. Thank you for sharing that experience with us. It not only provided us with a glimpse behind the scenes, but it also showcased the exceptional character and caliber of our coaches and this program. It was just one example of how you consistently make our families feel included and valued as part of this incredible experience."

In the same year, Jonathan Toczynski's high school basketball team experienced a tough season-ending loss. In such moments, it is often the parents who need to hear the reminders that true success is more than a result. As tears flowed from the athletes at the end of their season, Jonathan took a bold step by allowing the parents to address the team in the locker room. The parents spoke with pride, expressing their admiration for the boys' resilience throughout the season. It was a powerful reminder that there are values and growth that transcend mere numbers on a scoreboard.

These examples demonstrate the profound impact of including parents in postgame discussions. By fostering shared experiences, providing emotional support, and imparting valuable lessons, you transcend the narrow focus on wins and losses. You acknowledge the crucial role parents play in athletes' development and promote a culture of unity and mutual understanding among all stakeholders.

Look to Parents for Help

For some coaches, involving parents doesn't come naturally, like Coach Stephen Dale at St. Paul's School in Covington, Louisiana. However, Stephen recognizes the importance of parent involvement and encourages them to pass on the torch of parent leadership to each new group of parents. During one of their most successful seasons, the parents took the initiative to organize team gatherings and start a tradition of parent dinners on Friday nights. Led by a dedicated parent leadership group, they coordinated support for the team, arranged carpooling, and facilitated parent events.

There is something to be said for a strong parent community that bonds together, enjoys each other's company, and supports the team collectively, even without directly engaging with the team. In Chapter 5, I shared Nate Sanderson's insightful questions for parents at the start of the season:

➤ What do you want your experience to be like as a sports parent?

➤ What can you do for each other to help create that experience?

These questions have empowered parents to organize activities that involve everyone and develop their own traditions over the years. For example, a client of mine, Clint Halladay, stepped up to be a leader for his son's soccer team. Seeing that the coach wasn't organizing such events, Clint took it upon himself to coordinate activities like movie nights for the boys while the parents enjoyed dinner together. He also initiated book studies involving both parents and athletes.

Of course it's better not to have to wait for a parent to step up. That's why Nate designates a parent captain each season who not only assists with team logistics and coordinating parental involvement in the program but also takes the lead in organizing parent gatherings.

By looking to parents for help and encouraging their active involvement, coaches can create a vibrant community that extends beyond the field and nurtures a sense of camaraderie among all stakeholders.

TAKE ACTION

1. Seek chances to involve parents in team experiences, such as team meals, practices, or fun activities.

2. Invite parents to be a part of a team's pivotal moments, whether it's celebrating a significant victory or reflecting on a tough loss.

3. Don't feel like you have to handle all parent coordination yourself. Identify a willing parent or a group of parents who can take charge and help organize activities and support for the team. Delegate and empower them to contribute to the team's success.

CHAPTER 8

CREATE POWERFUL MOMENTS

n March 2018, the Indiana Wesleyan basketball team faced a pivotal moment after narrowly winning their "Sweet 16" game during the national tournament. Their dream of becoming national champions hinged on winning three games in the next four days. To make matters more challenging, their upcoming quarterfinals game was against a team that had already defeated them earlier in the year and eliminated them in the previous season's Final Four. Expectations were high for this group and the looming fear of repeating the previous season's defeat was weighing heavily on them. Coach Greg Tonagel was worried that his team would be playing afraid.

Rather than gathering with the team alone, Tonagel decided to bring the fathers into the equation. They all sat together in a hotel meeting room in a large circle, and Tonagel asked everyone, including the fathers, to write down their current fears or frustrations going into the game. These were the obstacles that hindered them from playing with the fearlessness and joy which had been their mission as a team that season. He then asked them to share their fears with the group.

One of the team's starters, Kyle Mangus, shared his fear that their opponent would play with more hunger. Captain Jacob Johnson worried that he wouldn't live up to the expectations of leading the team to a national championship, failing to continue the legacy of past leaders. The assistant coach responsible for scouting the opponents admitted his fear, believing that they were up against the best offense in the tournament. Through this exercise, both coaches and players identified the fears they were carrying. After sharing their fears, they symbolically threw them away together.

After this, one by one, the players stood up, and a powerful moment unfolded as the team, coaches, and fathers began to acknowledge and celebrate the greatness within each individual. They highlighted the qualities and specific instances where they had witnessed the players performing with true joy throughout the season. The energy in the room shifted, and everything clicked for the team the next day. They would start the game by taking an 8–0 lead and successfully hold off every comeback by their opponent. Filled with joy, they played without fear—not only that day but throughout the remainder of the tournament.

On the morning of the national championship, the fathers were once again invited to join the team for the morning film session. After reviewing the scout footage, players and coaches took a moment to reflect on their favorite moments and turning points of the season. The session concluded with an expression of gratitude, with every player, coach, and father completing the sentence, "Man, I got it good . . ." The team went on to win the championship game comfortably with a final score of 84–71.

The Power of Moments

Including fathers in intimate team moments at the final stages of the season may not seem surprising for Tonagel and his team, considering their involvement since the offseason retreat. But consistently involving them even during the national championship reinforces their connection and enhances the shared journey they have embarked upon. By including fathers in these moments, not only are the experiences for the athletes enhanced, but there is also a profound impact on the fathers themselves. As one father eloquently expressed, "To witness the culture being reinforced and lived is a transformative experience. It truly changed my life." By including parents in these special moments, they get to share in the unique experiences that the program offers its members. It is evident, time and time again, that when coaches embrace the presence of parents in these powerful junctures of the journey, they become more memorable and impactful than the games themselves.

Throughout this book, I have shared numerous stories of powerful moments, such as the father-son retreat, parent experience day, home visits, and personal letters to a sailor's father. While not every powerful moment needs to revolve around parents, this chapter offers additional ways for you to continue to create powerful moments with parents. Why are these moments so important? Research shows that when recalling experiences, we tend to forget most of what happens and instead focus on a few particular moments. As Dan and Chip Heath advocate in their book *The Power of Moments*, "Defining moments shape our lives, but we don't have to wait for them to happen."[11]

In today's world, technology and our fast-paced lives create obstacles to connecting and building relationships. Many parents find themselves increasingly isolated from their children. Family dinners are becoming rare, with everyone rushing around, engrossed in their phones, or glued to the television. Parents struggle to maintain relationships with their children and stay informed about their lives, and the dynamics only worsen once children go to college. A study conducted by the National Alliance on Mental Illness revealed a stark contrast in perceptions of mental health between parents and college students. While only 7 percent of parents reported their college students experiencing mental health issues, a staggering 50 percent of students rated their mental health as below average or poor. But powerful moments can help transform relationships and bridge the gap between parents and children.

In my experience, breaking away from the usual practice of excluding parents has consistently proven beneficial for both the team and the athletes. Each team has its own unique traditions and experiences that contribute to its identity. By inviting parents to be part of these moments during the season, we provide them with a glimpse into the team's culture and create an opportunity for them to share in their child's accomplishments. Offering them a moment to witness firsthand the dedication, camaraderie, and achievements of the team helps them gain valuable insights into their child's experiences and growth as an athlete. Here are some additional ideas for powerful moments you can create for parents.

Parent-Child Retreats

Inspired by Tonagel's approach, Nate VanDuyne wasted no time in scheduling a father-son retreat upon taking over the Brookwood

School basketball program in Georgia. The purpose of this retreat was to provide fathers with an opportunity to witness the program's values and operations while encouraging their support. One athlete shared with Nate he had never been a part of something like that with his father and would never forget how much fun they all had together. Multiple fathers let Nate know how much they appreciated the opportunity to see the program firsthand and experience the coaches' vision and the team's dynamic.

Organizing such an event may initially appear challenging, but as Tonagel has advised numerous coaches, simplicity is key. The retreat should offer good food, adventurous activities, and storytelling. You can incorporate any other team activities and allow parents to observe and participate in them.

It's also important to acknowledge that not every father or mother may be able to attend a retreat. Indiana Wesleyan has faced this challenge over the years with many of their international players. In such situations, Tonagel suggests seeking out mentors for these athletes throughout the season, with the retreat serving as an excellent opportunity to establish the foundation for those mentoring relationships.

Valentine's Day Dinner

Tim Trendel, the men's basketball coach of Providence Catholic in Chicago, had a unique goal in mind when he initiated the tradition of his team hosting a Valentine's Day dinner for their mothers. Beyond simply impressing the mothers, he recognized that many of his athletes struggled with fundamental skills surrounding respecting women during dates. His intention was to develop some of these dating skills, foster vulnerability among the players, and facilitate a reconnection between mothers and sons.

Each year around Valentine's Day, the athletes participate in this special event by dressing up and taking their mothers together on a date to a nice restaurant. Following the meal, each player honors their mother by standing up and reciting a heartfelt poem they wrote specifically for her. Tim was inspired to continue the tradition each year, witnessing mothers with tears in their eyes as their sons read the poems. Many mothers approached him after the dinner, expressing their gratitude and mentioning that it was the most they had spoken with their sons in months. Numerous teams have successfully replicated Tim's Valentine's Day Dinner with both mother-sons and father-daughters.

Parent Appreciation Night

Finding opportunities to express gratitude to parents for their unwavering support is an important aspect of coaching. One powerful way is through a parent appreciation night.

Each athlete selects a parent whom they wish to honor at one of the team's home games. Leading up to the event, the athlete takes the time to interview their chosen parent and delve into their experiences. The interview includes meaningful questions that allow the athletes to gain insights into their parents' journey.

Some of my favorite questions are these:

➤   What were some of your biggest fears and worries when you first became a parent?

- → What do you enjoy most about being a parent?
- → What are some of the most challenging aspects of being a parent?
- → What do you think is the most important thing you've learned about parenting?
- → What's something you wish you knew before becoming a parent?
- → What's the hardest decision you've had to make as a parent?
- → What do you think is the most important quality for a parent to have?
- → How do you balance being a parent with your other responsibilities and interests?

The day after the interview, the team comes together to discuss their findings and newfound understanding of parenting. They then individually write a heartfelt letter of appreciation to their parents, expressing gratitude for their love and support.

During the next game, either before or at halftime, the parents are honored. A short bio is read that the athletes have prepared about their parents, highlighting what makes them special and expressing their deepest appreciation. This heartfelt tribute serves as a powerful recognition of the parent's role in their child's life and the team's collective gratitude for their support.

TAKE ACTION

1. Start a parent-child bonding event, whether it's a retreat, special dinner, or a similar activity, to provide a dedicated space for quality time together.

2. Organize a parent appreciation night where athletes delve into their parents' experiences and gain insights into parenthood, culminating in an expression of gratitude for their support.

3. Keep thinking outside the box for opportunities to involve parents to create powerful moments of connection, like inviting them to be a part of a pregame film session or a team meeting.

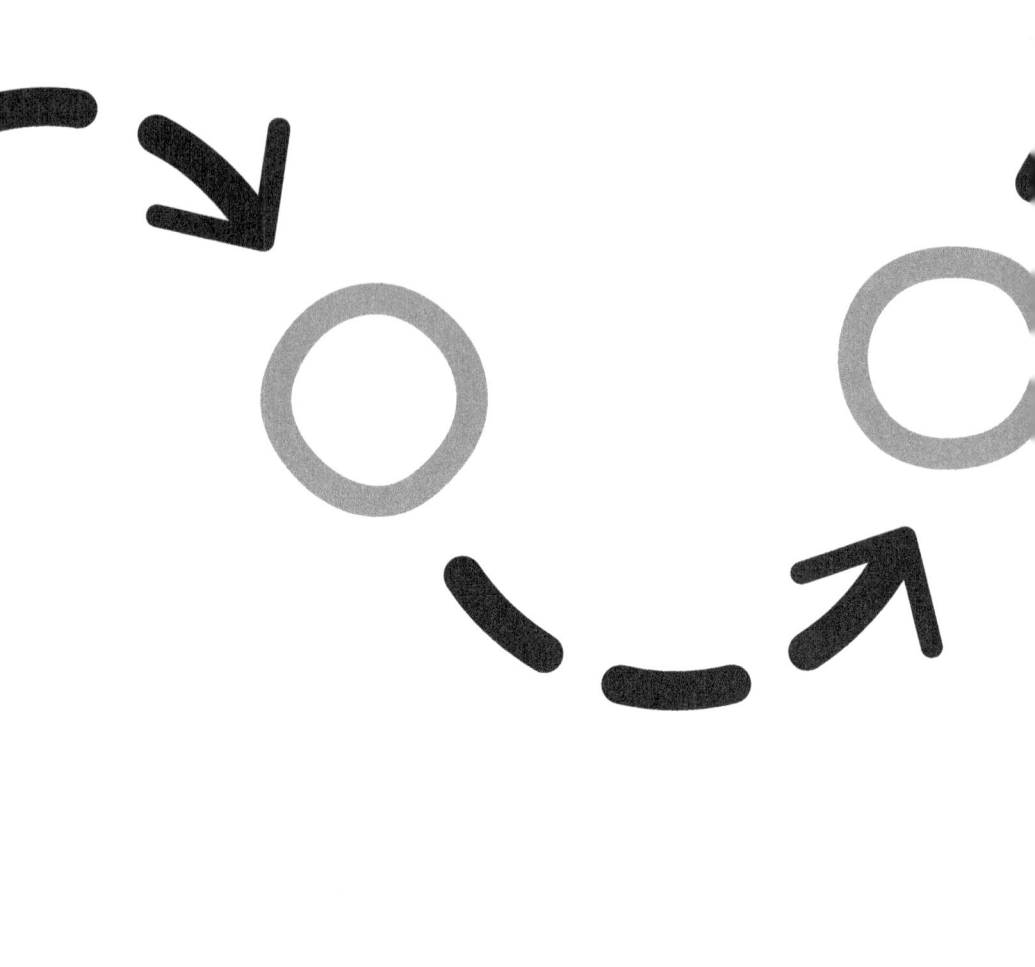

PART FOUR
ENFORCE THE CULTURE

In Part Four, we delve into a variety of strategies and skills for effectively handling conflicts with parents when they arise. Given the significant time, energy, and resources parents invest in supporting their child's athletic journey, combined with the competitive nature of sports, volatile situations can emerge.

Chapter 9 shares the eye-opening story of a college coach facing a disgruntled father, highlighting that dealing with unhappy parents is an unavoidable reality no matter how successful a coach may be. The chapter presents a valuable framework for engaging in difficult conversations productively to ensure parents feel heard and gain a broader perspective on the situation's complexity.

In Chapter 10, you'll encounter an all-too-common tale of a parent uprising against a coach. Failure to enforce boundaries can lead to a cultural breakdown and potentially cost a coach their job. This chapter offers guidance on collaborating with your administration to determine the most appropriate and effective methods for handling inappropriate parent behavior while safeguarding your mental and emotional well-being from the toxic and sometimes bullying behavior demonstrated by some parents today.

The application of these strategies is context-specific, allowing you (and possibly your administrator) to discern the most suitable times to employ certain approaches and develop the necessary skills to navigate conflicts effectively. The positive aspect is that these conflict management skills can be applied not only in coaching but in all aspects of life, ultimately making you a more effective and resilient leader.

ENGAGE IN HARD CONVERSATIONS

"**W**hy isn't my daughter playing more?!" The exclamation reverberated through Anson Dorrance's office the day after their national championship win. It wasn't a genuine question but an exclamation of anger. No answer Dorrance could provide that day would satisfy the irate father. The daughter in question, a junior athlete, had been a starter in every game as a sophomore, and the team struggled that season. In her junior year, Dorrance had reduced her role on the field, removing her from the starting lineup and limiting her playing time, particularly in the pivotal national championship game.

Dorrance was dumbfounded by the father's relentless questioning, trying to explain. "We tried that approach last year, and it didn't work. This year, we tried something different, and if you were there yesterday, you know that we are now national champions." Despite Dorrance repeating his reasoning, the father persisted, unsatisfied with his explanation. Dorrance's wife, who overheard the conversation from outside the office, couldn't believe it—Dorrance had said the same thing ten different ways before the father stormed out, unable to let go of his disappointment and with his anger unresolved.

The Hard Conversations

Coaches often encounter similar situations with irrational sports parents. These parents come to you with concerns regarding their child's playing time, disciplinary measures, conflicts with other players on the team, or a perception that you are not doing enough for their child's development. Now, not every parent who confronts you about an issue will be irrational; often they are just concerned, and you've potentially invited these conversations using some of the strategies mentioned earlier. Still, some parents will be just like that father and not ready to hear your reasoning. They've become entangled in their own narrative.

One of the most challenging aspects of working with these parents is that they are often unaware of being "that parent." You can even detect it in their request to meet. You might recognize some of these opening remarks in the text or email they send you:

"I'm not the kind of parent who contacts the coach, but . . ."

"I really appreciate everything you do, but . . ."

"I've been holding my tongue for as long as I can, but . . ."

"My child asked me not to say anything, but . . ."

As Dorrance explained to his wife that evening, "This is what it's like dealing with certain parents. They love their kids and don't want them to suffer. It's hard for them. But you cannot genuflect to their pressure." One of the qualities I admire about Dorrance is his ability to stand by his decisions while remaining open to conversations with parents. He acknowledges that these discussions are inevitable, regardless of the team's success. But he also believes (as I do) that these conversations are essential. Given the high degree of discomfort they produce, a logical question to ask is why a coach should think such conversations are essential?

First and foremost, these conversations are crucial to demonstrating care for the athlete and valuing the partnership with their parents. Conflict is a natural part of any relationship, and avoiding or prematurely terminating the relationship due to conflict is not an effective way to manage it. By listening to the parent's concerns, coaches show that they care about the athlete's well-being and respect the parent's perspective.

These conversations also provide valuable insights into the challenges the athlete may be facing in their home environment. It is important to distinguish between the perspectives of parents and children, and I consistently discover a disconnect between the two when working with the coaches I support. Frequently, athletes demonstrate their commitment and embrace their roles, while parents may not share the same viewpoint. This occurs because parents are not involved in the daily communication processes that the athletes experience, and young athletes aren't always the best communicators with their parents. Engaging in these conversations directly with the parent can help them understand what is happening and help us grasp the dynamic at home.

Another reason why I think coaches should welcome such conversations is the high value I place on fostering a healthy team culture. A coach who supports a healthy team culture can recognize the difference between being right and being effective. They may be completely right in their decisions regarding playing time and right in that they shouldn't have to explain those decisions to a particular parent. However, what does being right achieve in these situations? Parents are an integral part of the team culture, whether coaches like it or not, and a toxic parent can significantly alter the narrative within the team. Even if their narrative is based on falsehoods, it still reflects their feelings and perceptions. If parents don't share their concerns with coaches, they will likely share them with others, including their child, other parents, and administrators. It is far more preferable to be able to address those concerns directly versus having to do so through third parties. By listening to their story, you can not only address their concerns but also identify areas where you can make improvements to prevent future misunderstandings.

Lastly, these conversations are essential for helping parents. They don't know what they don't know. Every time a parent approaches you with an issue, you have an opportunity to coach them on what truly matters. When a parent expresses anger or frustration, ask them, "What is your biggest concern for your child?" This often opens up a conversation about their child as a person, not just as an athlete. It may reveal that their anxiety stems from deeper fears or concerns. These conversations provide a chance to educate and support parents in a meaningful way.

Inevitably, hard conversations will arise, and they hold significant importance. While each parent and situation are unique, I'd like to share a proven three-part framework for engaging in difficult conversations with parents. As noted before, my recommendation is that because they are the focus of the discussion, the athlete should be part of these conversations (in the next chapter we'll discuss the potential role an administrator might play in these conversations).

The Three Phases of Effective Hard Conversations

Phase 1: Actively Listen

Studies indicate that when individuals experience being heard, they are more inclined to reflect on their thinking and behaviors and exhibit receptiveness to different perspectives. Moreover, they display reduced defensiveness and resistance, making them more open to listening to others.

Rather than immediately formulating a response or explanation, begin the conversation with genuine curiosity. Focus on the other person and their words. Actively listen to what they say, paying attention to their expressions and emotions. During this phase, detach yourself from your agenda and perspective.

Former FBI negotiator Chris Voss, author of *Never Split the Difference*, teaches leaders to "engage with a mindset of discovery. Your goal at the outset is to extract and observe as much information as possible. Which, by the way, is one of the reasons that really smart people often have trouble being negotiators— they're so smart they think they don't have anything to discover."[12] You are trying to better understand not just their perspective but why they think the way that they do. You are trying to unearth the story they are telling themselves.

When you speak, start by asking curious questions and avoid leading questions. Leading questions inherently imply a predetermined "right" answer and lack genuine curiosity. They tend to elicit responses that align with the questioner's expectations, disguising their opinion within the question itself. Avoid questions like these:

→ We've given your child plenty of opportunities to prove themselves the last month. Why do you think they should be playing more?

→ As we discussed at the start of the year, not everybody is going to be happy with their playing time. Why are you not happy with your child's playing time?

Instead, utilize "what" questions rather than "why" questions to foster open and insightful discussions. "Why" questions often seek justification and can make individuals feel defensive, whereas "what" questions encourage exploration and forward-looking thinking. For example, you can ask these kinds of questions:

→ What would you like to discuss today that would be helpful for you and your child?

→ What are you noticing?

→ What's so important about that to you?

→ What reasons do you have for thinking and feeling that way?

→ What would be a good outcome?

→ What would be a good solution?

→ Tell me a little more about . . .

If unsure about the next step or follow-up question, sometimes embracing silence is the answer. Alternatively, you can practice reflective listening or mirroring. By paraphrasing and sharing back what the person has expressed, they feel heard and become more emotionally regulated. Summarize what you have understood, using phrases like "It sounds like . . ." or "What I think I've heard is . . ." Ask them, "Is there anything else I'm missing?" As Chris Voss teaches, you'll know they feel listened to when they respond with "That's right," rather than "You're right," indicating they feel understood.

When listening in this way, you not only uncover deeper insights into the issue they came to discuss but also help them become aware of what is at stake for them. In many instances, active listening alone has completely resolved issues between coaches and parents. As Philip Stanhope, the 4th Earl of Chesterfield, once said, "Many a man would rather you heard his story than grant his request."

Occasionally, parents may experience a breakthrough during this phase. I recall a coach sharing a humorous moment with me after a conversation with a parent. After about 10 minutes of active listening and asking curious questions, the mother had an "aha" moment and exclaimed, "I'm so sorry, I just realized I'm turning into that crazy parent! I can't believe I've taken up your time. This is for my son to learn to deal with. Thanks for listening to my nonsense." Not every parent will have this kind of realization, but they may be more receptive to Phase 2, where you share your perspective.

Phase 2: Share Your Perspective

Once the parent feels heard and understood, thank the parent for sharing and ask for permission to share your observations and the reasoning behind your decisions. This can be done by saying something like, "If it's all right, I'd like to share a bit of our perspective."

Before sharing your perspective, it can be helpful to use what Chris Voss calls an "accusation audit." Name the things the other parent could potentially accuse you of, such as the following:

➔ "I know I botched X . . ."
➔ "I haven't done a good job at . . ."
➔ "I know I didn't communicate . . ."
➔ "We tried X, Y, and Z, and it didn't work . . ."
➔ "That was bad coaching . . ."

The key to disarming the other person is to vocalize their potential objections first by owning them (to a degree) and then following with something like,

➔ "My intention was to . . ."
➔ "I meant to communicate . . ."
➔ "I did X, Y happened, and now here's where we are . . ."

Sometimes it might be worthwhile to acknowledge some particular challenges associated with the situation for the coach (for example, it might be early in the season, and you are still in the figuring-it-out stage of the rotation).

As we have discussed throughout this book, it is essential to lead this phase with conviction. There is no need to sugarcoat the reality of the situation. Be candid about the reasons behind your decisions. If it's a discussion about playing time, it could be that their child is simply not performing better than other players ahead of them. If it's a discipline issue, their child may have engaged in negative behavior that requires accountability. If it's a development concern, their child may not be taking responsibility for their own growth. Be clear and concise in your assessment, avoiding labels such as "lazy," "entitled," or "bad teammate." Instead, focus on sharing behavioral observations and evidence, such as consistently showing up late, displaying poor effort in drills, or failing to help teammates.

It's important to connect the conversation back to earlier one-on-one and parent meetings, referencing what you and the parents previously shared. For example, you might say, "I remember in our meeting at the start of the season, you expressed concern for your daughter's mental health. You mentioned that she gets overstressed in life, and you want her to develop better coping skills. Giving her more playing time is not the solution, as we both know she will face more adversity in life down the road. This is an opportunity for growth."

Another example related to discipline could be, "I understand that it's difficult for your son to sit out during games. It's difficult for us too, because we want him on the field. However, he knows the standards of this team and the consequences of his actions. He will continue to sit out if he chooses to complain to referees and criticize his teammates." This is where the earlier work done in parent meetings can truly pay off. Reminding them of the agreements made in your partnership is immensely beneficial, especially as you bring the conversation back to the concept of a partnership in Phase 3.

Phase 3: Partner for Success

In Phase 3, clarify the actions you and the parents will take moving forward. At times, you may recognize areas where you could have done better and take responsibility for those things. This may involve addressing communication issues or acknowledging instances where you may have lost your composure and handled a situation inappropriately. In many cases, you will need to stand your ground on the decisions you have made.

During this phase, try asking questions like, "What's the best way for us to move forward?" or "What can we both do to support your child moving forward?" Using inclusive language like "we" instead of "you" emphasizes the partnership. As the parents share their next steps, inquire about the support they need from you.

Parents may make requests that you are unwilling or unable to fulfill or that may be unhelpful for you to undertake. At this point, it is necessary to establish boundaries (which will be discussed in the next chapter) and communicate, "I'm sorry, but that's not something I am willing or able to do for you and your child." Whatever you are committed to doing as a coach to support the athlete, be sure to verbalize it clearly for the parents and the athlete (if they are present).

Ultimately, the goal of the conversation is for the parent to feel heard, gain new insights or perspectives into the situation, and establish a clear path forward.

The Impact of Difficult Conversations

In his first year as head coach at Woodbridge High School in New Jersey, Jonathan Toczynski brought a lot of change to the basketball program's culture. One significant change was how playing time was earned, emphasizing behavioral standards and not relying solely on seniority. It was bound to rock the boat, especially when the team got off to a rocky start with three consecutive losses. Still, Jonathan remained committed to the culture of high standards, even though it meant reducing playing time for two twin seniors on his team who failed to meet their standard of no blaming, complaining, or defending.

Dissatisfied with the new coach's approach, the father of the twins contacted the school administration. A meeting was scheduled involving Jonathan, the parents, the principal, and the athletic director. Recognizing this as an important moment, Jonathan and I reviewed the framework for hard conversations. Going into the meeting, he began with an accusation audit, acknowledging his unconventional methods and the potential perception that he did not value the seniors. Then, he posed the question, "What issues or concerns do you have?" And then he shut up and listened.

The father expressed his disagreement with Jonathan's focus on culture and character, insisting that winning should take precedence. He shared his disapproval of the team's activities, such as community service and the daily personal development reading and discussion, deeming them as time wasted. He let Jonathan know he thought he was a joke and embarrassing the boys.

After listening to the father's 15-minute rant, Jonathan summarized what he had heard and asked if there was anything else he had missed. Once the father confirmed that was all, Jonathan shared his perspective. He acknowledged the players' strengths but highlighted areas for improvement. He emphasized that he would not compromise culture for winning and explained the rationale behind team reading and community service, rooted in care and developing perspective and gratitude. Jonathan concluded by saying, "This is how I plan to build the culture here and I understand that will not be for everyone. That's okay."

Although the parents did not immediately change their opinion, the meeting allowed Jonathan to demonstrate his conviction and vision to the administrators present. Moving forward, Jonathan asked how he could best support their two sons. The parents had little to say at that moment as they seemed taken aback by the strength and conviction of the new coach. Jonathan stayed true to his principles as a leader, and the parents decided to withdraw their sons from the team only two games later.

Despite the unfortunate outcome for the two players, the team benefited and went on to form a strong brotherhood able to withstand the adversity and challenges of a season that would destroy other team cultures. Future seniors and all athletes learned that regardless of how talented an athlete is, the standard is the standard and that they would be held accountable to it. The parent culture has shifted to one of support, with parents rallying behind the young coach. And the best part is Jonathan didn't have to compromise winning for the sake of the team culture. Despite starting 0–5, the team came together after the twins left the team and finished the season with a strong record of 8–9, winning twice as many games as they lost from that point forward. The success continued into the following season, where they achieved an overall winning record while maintaining the standard Jonathan wanted to see.

Even if it doesn't always result in agreement, using the framework for difficult conversations helps to create a calm and respectful atmosphere. It allows the other person to feel understood, enabling them to make a well-informed decision about whether they are in the right place or if they should explore alternatives that align better with their priorities.

↳ TAKE ACTION

1. Embrace hard conversations with parents as an opportunity for growth and understanding. Engage in active listening by adopting a curious mindset. Ask open-ended "what" questions instead of leading or "why" questions. Embrace moments of silence and use reflective listening techniques to show you understand their perspective.

2. When sharing your perspective, begin by conducting an accusation audit, acknowledging any areas where they may feel you fell short. Avoid using labels for their child and instead focus on sharing your behavioral observations. Connect the current conflict to earlier conversations with parents, reminding them of the agreements and standards established.

3. Partner with the parents to identify actionable steps that both parties can take moving forward. Take responsibility for any areas where you can improve as a leader while maintaining conviction in your decisions. Use inclusive language like "we" to emphasize shared responsibility.

CHAPTER 10

ENFORCE BOUNDARIES

The athletic director slid the letter across the desk toward Nate Sanderson, the head girls basketball coach at Linn-Mar High School, and said, "I need you to resign for personal reasons." The letter had been written for him, lacking only his signature to take effect. With nine games left in his third season on the job, Nate was out.

He was stunned, saddened, but not surprised. The pressure had been building for weeks. The team was underachieving, and Nate's confidence was shot. Sleep was hard to come by as they struggled to overcome a desperate shooting slump. Upperclassmen were irate for being out of the rotation. Parents were up in arms. The mental and emotional burden was unlike anything he or his family had ever experienced.

How did it come to this?

In 2017, Nate accepted the head girls basketball position at Linn-Mar High School after winning back-to-back state championships the previous two seasons at Springville High School. The new job was a promising one, with multiple Division I athletes on the roster when he took over. However, that would not last.

From the time he took the job in June to the first day of practice in November, 17 athletes decided not to play basketball. Their reasons varied, but the departures gutted their roster, and they finished that first season with the worst record in school history, winning just three games. The common refrain from the critics was, "This small school approach won't work at a big school."

In Year Two they made significant progress, finishing the season on a five-game winning streak before losing to the defending state champions in the postseason. They pushed their record to 11–10 that year, and with only one senior on the roster, expectations were high going into Year Three. In fact, their third season started with one of the best weeks of practice Nate had ever been a part of.

Then, adversity struck. The team really struggled to shoot the ball to open the season. Despite improvements in nearly every other statistical category, their inability to put the ball in the basket equated to a 2–5 start before the break. With a team that probably should have been 5–2, they were underachieving and the vultures were circling.

Players and their parents began voicing their dissatisfaction with their playing time, sometimes to Nate but more often to the administration. In spite of this, he held firm to his belief that playing time should be earned rather than a rite of passage as one became an upperclassman.

Tensions continued to escalate. Nate's friends complained of the toxic parent environment in the stands. Anonymous letters arrived with suggestions about the offense, the rotation, and who should be dressing varsity. Nate endured what he refers to as the "Parent Meeting from Hell," as one of the senior parents requested a meeting with the coaching staff and athletic director. For 90 minutes they listened as they went through a four-page bulleted list of all their complaints from his three years of coaching their daughter.

And just when it seemed like it couldn't get any worse, it did. Prior to Christmas break, he received a foreboding email from his athletic director asking to meet with him and his assistant before they returned to practice. For six days he was left dangling in the wind, wondering if his tenure was coming to a premature end. The AD had met with each individual player to solicit their opinion on how things were going and what changes needed to be made. Once again, he sat down and discussed another long list of complaints. It became difficult to trust people without knowing where the complaints were coming from. Players and captains were not forthcoming in their individual meetings with the coaching staff, yet were quick to complain behind closed doors to the administration.

To make matters worse, instead of fostering constructive dialogue, the athletic director delivered the list of grievances without offering much support when they were aired. Suddenly, with doubts about who said what, it became nearly impossible for Nate to have even simple conversations with players as he was haunted by the uncertainty of what was being said behind his back.

Desperate to salvage the season, he turned to the captain's council to collaborate on solutions to some of the most common complaints. That proved fruitless, as he later learned that the captains and their parents were intimately involved with the campaign to remove him as coach. Nevertheless, changes were made. He stopped conducting mental health days, a staple of his programs for years. He abandoned culture-building activities. Team dinners became players only. As a coaching staff, they focused all of their energy solely on helping the team win games.

Despite all the negativity, they continued to be competitive. They beat a crosstown rival by 30 points in a game where nearly everyone scored. They nearly upset the number one team in the state at their place before falling short late in the fourth quarter. After the game, the disappointment was palpable in the locker room. For some, it was because they came so close. For others, it was because they didn't play in the game.

No matter how well they were competing, the criticisms continued. The athletic director began making suggestions about rotations, timeouts, and style of play. It was made clear to Nate that the coaches should find a way to play the upperclassmen regardless of ability. Parents continued to register their complaints via emails and phone calls to the AD while players coordinated their complaints to maximize their effect.

Then he received an invitation from the AD for their "weekly meeting" (something that they never formally had). After staying home with a sick child that morning, he entered the athletic office and walked into an ambush: the letter lay on the desk, waiting for his signature. Parents had organized and threatened to boycott Senior Night and the banquet at the end of the year. At least "half a dozen" players threatened to transfer if he remained the head coach. Cornered by the mob, the AD capitulated and asked him to resign.

Just like that, the thing Nate loved to do more than anything else in this world was taken away from him. He was instructed to leave the building immediately. He would not be allowed to meet with the team, nor was he supposed to have any communication with his assistants. He was to simply disappear.

The Importance of Enforcing Boundaries

Nate's story highlights the struggles and betrayals that coaches can face in their coaching journey. Unfortunately, Nate's story is not unique; it has become increasingly common for parent uprisings to occur, with administrators often giving in to their demands. Coaches who have dedicated so much to their programs are often discarded and left to grapple with feelings of rejection, unwarranted criticism, and personal attacks. These moments don't just impact the coach; they also have a profound effect on their families, as their spouses and children are part of the community as well.

Regardless of what you do, you may encounter some parents who aren't just irrational but who are willing to do almost anything to secure what they want for their child. I have witnessed parents fabricating completely false stories to tarnish a coach's reputation and push them out. I have seen parents openly bashing their child's coach on social media. I have observed parents organizing secret meetings with other parents to strategize their efforts in forcing a coach out. I have even seen parents send hateful and bullying texts to coaches and their spouses.

In these situations, what can you do? You must enforce boundaries.

While it is important to be open to feedback and concerned about different perspectives and feelings, remember that you too are a human being deserving of respect. Even the most ineffective coach deserves to be treated kindly for dedicating their time. No one should be subjected to bullying. It is critical for you and your administrators to draw a line in the sand. You must enforce boundaries and be prepared to say, "Enough is enough." You must continue to coach with conviction and do what you believe is best for the team.

Often, these parents are carrying their own pain, unfulfilled dreams, or personal issues. However, we cannot allow them to make their issues our own. In those moments, it will require a great deal of courage. In this chapter, I share principles and strategies to help you protect your team and yourself from not only unhealthy but even toxic and harmful behavior from certain parents.

Clarify Administrative Support

In my work with coaches, I often assist them in preparing for job interviews, and one of the most important reminders I give them is that you aren't just being interviewed but are interviewing as well. Do you really want the job? What is it like to coach in that community? What are the expectations of you as a coach? What are the expectations of parents? Take the opportunity to ask your potential future boss, "What do you do to support your coaches when they face parent criticism?" You can even present a scenario you might have experienced in the past: "How would you handle it if a parent did X?" While it may not be a dealbreaker if they don't have a great answer, at least you will have an understanding of the level of support you can expect if things become difficult for you during a season.

A good rule of thumb is to overcommunicate with your administrators. As Carl Pierson discusses in his book *The Politics of Coaching*, administrators don't like surprises.[13] You are more likely to receive support when they are aware of issues before they are contacted by a parent. That might mean blind copying them on emails with parents or giving them a heads-up when you anticipate an interaction with a disgruntled parent or player. It's much harder for an administrator to support the coach when they are playing catch-up or first hearing about a problem from the parent.

As you are likely to make changes in your approach with parents after reading this book, it would be beneficial to sit down with your administrator and discuss the steps you plan to take in fostering better parent partnerships moving forward. Take the time to explain what you will be trying and why you are doing it, but don't hesitate to ask administrators about their role in parent-coach conflicts. Some administrators may take a hands-off approach and expect the coach to handle such situations. Others may see themselves as protectors of the coach and may handle complaints and criticisms without sharing them to spare the coach unnecessary worry. Yet others may view themselves as protectors of enrollment, public perception of the athletic program, and the athletic budget, which could lead to them swiftly cutting ties with a coach upon receiving a few complaints in their email inbox.

Most administrators have good intentions and may have been coaches themselves, so they may be just as puzzled as you were before reading this book about how to handle irate parents. Collaborate with your administrator to develop a game plan for managing conflict, because no matter how successful you are or how well you build partnership with parents, criticism will inevitably arise at some point in your coaching career.

Give Parents Feedback

In his book *The Parents We Mean to Be*, Richard Weissbourd presents two challenges for parents and educators in helping to raise moral human beings.[14] The first is to create strong connections among parents, which has been a central theme throughout this book. The second challenge is even more radical: give parents feedback. The same is true for coaches.

As you open yourself up to feedback from parents, they are more likely to be open to hearing your own observations and feedback. While it may not always be successful, I agree with Weissbourd that we should strive to share our feedback with parents more often. In these conversations, we can openly share what we notice or hear from parents and discuss the impact it has on the team and their child. It's important to have these conversations before the next step of enforcing consequences.

To initiate this conversation, find an appropriate time to speak with the parent privately and aim to be as nonjudgmental as possible. Here is a suggested framework.

Step 1: Notification

"Hey, can we chat? Lately, I think I have been hearing/seeing/noticing X, which is not in line with how we want any athlete, coach, or parent to behave in our program. I could be completely wrong, so please let me know if I am. I know you have high expectations and care deeply about your child and the team. I'm just trying to create a great experience for everyone and help this team be successful in the right way."

"X" represents the specific behavior you have observed. Some examples of behaviors you might identify include

➜   hearing the parent at games criticizing the referees, your coaching, and the athletes;

→ seeing the parent being hard on their child after games for their performance;

→ hearing rumors they are talking poorly about your coaching and the program; or

→ noticing that they reach out frequently when their child doesn't get much playing time.

Step 2: Actively Listen

Use the same skills and methods of active listening discussed in Chapter 9.

Step 3: Explore Natural Consequences with Questions

Don't hesitate to ask challenging questions, like those below, that prompt reflection on their behavior:

→ How do you think this behavior is affecting your child and the team?

→ How do you think it's impacting my ability to do my job?

→ What lessons do you think it teaches your child?

→ What message does it send to others in the community?

→ How do you think it affects your child's chances of recruitment?

→ You can never predict how these conversations will unfold or what will come out of them. However, they have a better chance of being successful if you have done the groundwork in building a positive relationship. Engaging in these conversations provides an opportunity to address concerns and potential misunderstandings in an open dialogue before resorting to disciplinary measures.

Use Logical Consequences with Parents

In my work with coaches, I emphasize the use of logical consequences with athletes as a means of enforcing standards and holding them accountable for their actions. Logical consequences follow the four Rs as outlined by Dr. Jane Nelsen, the founder of *Positive Discipline*: related, respectful, reasonable, and revealed in advance.[15] The same principles should apply to parents. Unfortunately, parents often face no consequences for their behavior. Coaches and administrators allow them to act inappropriately in the stands and on social media, permitting them to become a detriment to team culture. Here are some examples of potential logical consequences for parents:

1. *End of Conversation*: When a parent becomes emotional, disrespectful, or aggressive in a conversation, you may decide to end the discussion at that moment and revisit it later when emotions have subsided.

2. *Loss of Opportunity to Meet*: If a parent repeatedly displays disrespectful behavior or fails to take responsibility for their actions, you may choose to inform them that you will only communicate with the athlete moving forward, effectively ending the partnership.

3. *Loss of Privilege as a Fan*: Regardless of the financial contributions or support they provide, no parent is entitled to attend a sporting event if they continue to behave disrespectfully in the stands. At some point, they should lose the privilege to attend games.

4. *Removal of Child from the Team*: Coaches and administrators may be apprehensive about taking this step, as they believe

a child should not suffer due to their parents' actions. However, if you communicate this consequence beforehand and provide the parent an opportunity to correct their behavior, it is the parent who is ultimately choosing for their child to suffer. You have a responsibility to the team and the community to remove toxic parents, and sometimes the only way to do this is to remove the athlete from the team as well.

If your program has a history of unacceptable parent behavior, it may be necessary to communicate these consequences early in the year during your parent meeting. Another approach is to involve parents when creating a parent code of conduct or establishing parent standards at the beginning of the year. Ask them for input on what they believe are reasonable consequences when they fail to meet the established standards. Depending on your specific situation, it may be your responsibility or that of your administration to enforce these consequences—which is why it is crucial to have that important first conversation with your administration to clarify their support.

If you're fortunate, you'll have an administrator like Al Baker at Woodstock High School in Illinois, who doesn't hesitate to uphold and enforce boundaries. One of his head coaches received some abusive texts from a parent, blaming the coach for their daughter not making the all-conference team and even suggesting the coach should quit. Al promptly intervened, firmly informing the parent that such behavior was unacceptable. He made it clear that the parent would not be granted a meeting with the head coach or any administrator, and, as a consequence for sending such a text, would not be allowed to attend his daughter's games for the time being.

It is encouraging to witness administrators like Baker taking a strong stance in defending their coaches from insults and attacks from parents. We can only hope that more administrators follow suit and continue to support their coaching staff.

Build Your Internal Fortress

Throughout the years, I have witnessed some coaches maintain a high level of stoicism and ride out seasons of criticism. They seem capable of blocking out negativity and accepting it as part of the job. On the other hand, there are coaches (like myself) who are more easily affected by criticism. Negative parent emails, interactions, or even rumors of disgruntled parents would keep me up at night.

Ideally, my aspiration is to become a coach who can ignore things that won't matter in a week, calmly address valid criticisms, and maintain emotional and mental resilience. As the serenity prayer goes, "Grant to us the serenity of mind to accept that which cannot be changed, courage to change that which can be changed, and wisdom to know the one from the other." It's a prayer that all of us can probably relate to at some point and an area where all leaders can continue to grow.

In difficult moments I often remind coaches of a few things:

➜ Criticism is a sign that people care.
➜ It pays to be a little deaf and choose not to hear every criticism.
➜ Others' behavior toward us says more about who they are than who we are.

In addition to these principles, there are other ways to strengthen your internal defenses.

Build Healthy Routines

Many coaches refrain from checking their emails after games to protect their sleep. It's also helpful to limit social media use during the season. Taking care of yourself by eating well, exercising, getting enough sleep, and spending time with loved ones widens your window of tolerance.

Write a Hot Letter

Abraham Lincoln had a practice that he called the "hot letter." Whenever he felt the urge to confront someone, he would write a letter, pouring all his anger and frustration into it. However, instead of sending it, he would set it aside until his emotions subsided. On the letter, he would write, "Never sent. Never signed."

This method allows you to privately express your frustrations and feel heard without causing damage or facing backlash that speaking those words might lead to. Oftentimes, we tend to turn to our assistant coaches to vent these frustrations. While some may argue that it's a part of their role to listen to us vent, I respectfully disagree. Let's set a higher standard for ourselves and avoid spending too much time complaining and whining to our assistants about parents, athletes, or any other matters and write a hot letter instead.

Get a Coach or Mentor

Hiring a leadership coach was a transformative experience for me as a coach. Coaches have one of the most publicly criticized jobs that exist. Working with someone helped give me distance, gain new perspectives, and process criticism or conflict in a healthy manner. One of the reasons I started my business TOC was to provide that kind of one-on-one leadership support for sports coaches.

Keep a Sense of Humor

Using a lighthearted, joking tone with parents regarding their sometimes outrageous behavior at games can also be a gentle way to provide feedback or reminders. For instance, I would ask a parent named Phil, who often crossed boundaries, "Did you leave 'crazy Phil' at home today?"

One coach I know jokingly referred to his coaching staff as his "security team" when they walked out of the locker room together to fend off any parent assaults. Another coach I know would give funny awards to athletes and parents at the end of the season, such as a whistle to the parent who frequently criticized referees or a book on meditation to the father who always got extremely angry during games. Humor serves as a reminder to parents and ourselves that it's just a game.

Know When to Walk Away

Tyler Pearson, the head boys basketball coach at Highland High School in Idaho, knew he was in for a challenging journey as a coach. During a parent meeting, a parent had written on the expectations notecard, "Stop worrying about building character, just focus on winning some basketball games." Unfortunately, this parent's attitude represented around 20 percent of the parents' perspective in the program—a perspective that prioritized winning above all else. These parents preferred a coach who would scream, yell, and humiliate their sons to drive them to play hard, rather than working with athletes to develop their own motivation and sense of purpose within the team.

However, Tyler stayed true to his principles as a leader and continued to work diligently. Along the way, he gained the respect and support of many parents and the administration. Sadly, as the years went by, a particular group of families in the community refused to relent. The bullying texts, the coach-bashing to their sons and in the stands never ended. In that small Idaho community, the situation became too much for Tyler and his family. He made the difficult decision to step down as the head boys basketball coach, and the wounds ran deep enough that they decided to leave town.

There may come a point where you, like Nate and Tyler, realize that you are not what the community wants, and staying would require you to compromise your principles or your own well-being. The path forward may not exist or may not be worth pursuing. You have a greater responsibility to yourself and your family than you do to your athletes. In most of these situations, coaches experience relief as time passes, finding new communities that better align with their values as leaders, just like Tyler and Nate did in their new coaching opportunities. Experiencing challenges like this does not mean the end of a coaching career. It's essential to recognize that stepping away takes more courage than stubbornly remaining in a situation out of pride.

Know When to Hold Your Ground

Brennan Malone, the head track coach at Perry Central High School in Indiana, faced an intense situation that would test even the most convicted coaches. The team's star runner and three-sport athlete missed a week of practice, rendering him ineligible to compete according to the team standards cocreated and agreed upon at the beginning of the year.

The athlete's frustration escalated when he skipped the next track meet in protest, resulting in further suspension. To complicate matters, the athlete's mother was furious, believing the head coach was unfairly making an example of her son. Initial attempts to explain the team's standards and the coach's role in enforcing them didn't yield positive results.

The situation intensified when the mother reached out to the athletic director, threatening to transfer her son if he couldn't participate in the next meet. Despite having the support of his administration, Brennan felt the pressure to give in to the parent's demands. However, he recognized the cultural importance of upholding boundaries and teaching valuable life lessons to the young man.

Brennan decided he wouldn't yield to the pressure, but would address the issue with love and understanding. He invited the mother and her son to his home for dinner. Instead of dwelling on the matter at hand, the dinner conversation remained light and friendly, with no mention of sports or consequences.

After dinner, Brennan asked them to first share their perspectives, as he was there to listen and understand. After they had both gotten everything off their chest, he shared his own perspective. This candid exchange allowed the young athlete to realize the coach's genuine concern for him and the team's culture. While the mother didn't fully agree with the consequences, she respected Brennan's efforts to reconnect with her son.

This moment proved to be transformative for the young athlete. He not only accepted the consequences but became more motivated and dedicated, displaying newfound leadership and coachability throughout the remainder of the season. While the mother may not have fully appreciated the situation at that moment, it is likely that she will eventually recognize and value the moment when Brennan held her son accountable while expressing genuine care and concern.

→ TAKE ACTION

1. When considering a coaching job, interview the organization to gauge their administrative support, specifically regarding handling parent criticism.

2. Initiate constructive conversations with parents to give them feedback and use logical consequences for parents' inappropriate behavior. Communicate these consequences early and collaborate with your administration for support in enforcing them.

3. Build your internal fortress as a coach by valuing constructive criticism, focusing on self-care through healthy routines, finding a private outlet for frustrations, seeking guidance from a coach or mentor, and maintaining a sense of humor to navigate challenging situations. Recognize when it's necessary to walk away from a coaching position if the community's values clash with your principles.

CONCLUSION

It's a dry spring morning in Ireland, and I'm standing on the sideline watching my daughter Alena. At the time, she was only six years old, playing in her fourth-ever Gaelic football match. Just before the COVID-19 pandemic, we moved to Ireland to make a new life for our family in a small town outside of Dublin. Gaelic football, Ireland's most popular sport reaching all the way back to 1802 and not to be confused with soccer, is a truly Irish experience. Among all the activities we've enrolled her in over the years—dance, gymnastics, tennis, and basketball—this is the one I am probably rooting for the most, hoping she develops an interest and passion. The sport is not only exciting and physical but also an integral part of Irish culture and community.

Up until this point, she has shown little interest in sports. She mostly turns up to play with her friends and do cartwheels in the grass. And if the weather is cold and rainy, which it often is, playing with dolls is far more appealing.

But today something is different. She seems enthusiastic and energized. Whether it's the weather, a good night's sleep, or a hearty breakfast, I am not sure. But it's as if a switch was flipped in her mind, and from the get-go, she is fully engaged in the game and eager to compete. Considering half of the girls on the field still don't have a clue what they are doing, and the fact that she is her father's daughter (tall and fairly athletic), she quickly stands out as she sprints all over the field, making tackles, stealing the ball, running down the field, and scoring points. With each point she scores, I get a hit of dopamine and my excitement grows. I struggle to contain my joy on the sideline, attempting to maintain a stoic presence, never wanting to be "that parent." On that day, she was the best player on the field and I loved watching her play. Deep down, I was hoping this was a breakthrough for her.

As I drove her home, I reflected on watching my daughter play so well and the joy I experienced. Without a doubt, I was genuinely happy to see her having fun and gaining confidence. But in that moment, I became aware of a few other truths.

First, it feels really good to see our kids perform well. It was almost as if I was scoring those points myself. This made me wonder how much different the feeling was for Michael Jordan making a game-winner as opposed to the feeling his father, James Jordan, had? Did Earl Woods feel the same rush of joy when Tiger sunk a big-time putt? And what about the countless other sports parents I had criticized over the years?

Second, a part of me wanted a child who reminded me of myself as a kid: driven and passionate to become the best I could be at my sport. Since moving on from basketball, I have spent many hours thinking, "What if?" What if I knew then what I know now? How much further could I have gotten? How much better could I have become? I started to realize how easy it was for parents to use their children to pursue unfulfilled dreams.

In fact, on the car ride home, I became acutely aware of how easy it could be to become the sports parent I dread. Since having children, I had sworn I'd never be the type of sports parent who posted about my child's achievements on social media and bragged about their accomplishments at social functions. I promised myself I would never be the sports parent who couldn't keep his mouth shut on the sideline. I would never be the one coaching my kids in the car ride home, bringing up sports every night at dinner, or planning our entire life around their sporting schedule. And there was no way I would become the sports parent so invested in my child's sports career that I end up wanting success more than they do.

Heck, I wasn't even sure I wanted my kids in sports. It's not that I don't see the benefits of sports; I've experienced them in my own life as well as in the lives of countless others. Sports have the potential to strengthen our character, develop healthy relationships, and be a source of joy for a family. I've witnessed how sports can unite a community, instill pride, and create great memories. My best friend in life came from sports; our deep bond was forged in a basketball gym during a hot summer, pushing each other to improve.

Yet, I also know the darker side of sports. I know what it can do to a young person—I've seen it in myself and countless others. The constant comparison to peers and the pressure to perform can take a toll. Sports can quickly become all-consuming, and the joy that comes from play can be lost in the blink of an eye. The purity of the game becomes tarnished with ambitions for scholarships, contracts, and improved status. Perhaps the most dangerous aspect of sports is the all-too-common trap for athletes to believe that their value and self-worth are somehow connected to how well they can shoot, kick, or hit a ball. And so I had my hesitations to sign my kids up for sports.

Every parent begins with the intention for their kids to have fun, be happy and healthy, and grow from the experience of playing sports. However, when you put 30 kids on the field with a ball, ask them to compete, keep score, and surround them with fans, most of us start wanting something a little more for our kids. We want them to not only do well, but we also yearn to believe that our kids are special, different, and extraordinary—not just like the other 29 kids on the field. My son Kieran was only born for five minutes before these ideas of him being special started to come up for me. After the nurse measured his feet and told me I could expect him to be very tall, my first thought was, "Maybe he has a future in the NBA!"

Becoming a sports parent has deepened my empathy for sports parents to a whole new level that I could never reach in my 15 years of coaching. Now I see how easy it can be for everything to get out of balance. I hope this book will help coaches better partner with parents, ensuring both coaches and parents keep their ambition and passion in check—never sacrificing what is most important on the altar of achievement. Perhaps one day, this book will also help a coach support me as a sports parent.

We live in a difficult time where social media and the growing money in sports have driven coaches, athletes, and parents to become more inwardly focused on what they can get out of sports. Sports have become less about who you are becoming through the journey or sacrificing with others for a common goal. We need parents and coaches to work together to restore sports to a healthy place in our culture. As you move forward, I want to extend these three challenges to every coach.

Challenge 1: Hold Compassion for Parents

As I have come to realize from personal experience, parenting is one of our greatest challenges in life. Parenting in today's sporting environment is even more overwhelming. Most everyone is doing the best they can with what they know. Before we judge parents harshly and erect walls, let's remember parents are human beings and have their own problems.

Challenge 2: Love Your Athletes

As Anson Dorrance says, "There are a thousand ways to love your athletes other than giving them playing time." Whether the parents see it or not, it's up to you as a coach to find ways to demonstrate that love to each and every athlete. It might be five years before they express gratitude for your efforts, like the story I told in the introduction about Danny's father. Some parents may never recognize it. But what matters is that you know you cared, treated the athlete with respect, and valued them. As much as coaches want the parents to recognize it and be grateful, they most importantly want the athlete to know it—to know they were seen, known, and loved.

Challenge 3: Lead with Courage

Let's stop looking to others in the world for the leadership we so desperately need. Let's be that leader. Parents need leadership, and that leader can be you. It can be easy for us to play it safe, to keep our mouths shut, whether we are the coach on the sideline or parent in the stands. It's easy to give in to the fear of taking risks, trying something new, or speaking up. It's terrifying to call parents and educate them on where they are falling short and how to improve.

Maybe you need to be a coach like Clint Halladay, who takes the time to organize an event for athletes to connect off the field, like going to the movies while parents on the team grab dinner. Perhaps it's trying something new, like Tim Trendel hosting a Valentine's dinner with your athletes and their mothers. At some point, we all need to have the courage of Jonathan Toczynski, who engaged with angry parents with an open mind, listened, and then shared his perspective with conviction.

As you do these things, sometimes parents will love it and be grateful for the work you do. Sometimes they might reject it and tell you to get back into your lane, as they did with Tyler Pearson, or they might even run you out of town, as they did with Nate Sanderson. There are no guarantees of success in every relationship—that's leadership.

Leadership therefore requires vulnerability—to step forward, put yourself out there in relationships, and be willing to take risks in order to make things better. You must have the courage and willingness to engage rather than sitting back on the sidelines and merely criticize the current state of affairs.

———————————————

Many times, I think back to May 2012. After nearly six years of coaching basketball, I had decided to leave Ireland to move to America to be closer to my girlfriend at the time, who would later become my wife. My friends decided to throw me quite the goodbye party, with food, a band, and a DJ. Irish people love parties; as they often joke, they'd celebrate the opening of an envelope. My friends knew how important my players were in my life, so they were all invited along with their parents to send me on my way.

As the night came to a close, the DJ played the final song, John Denver's "Take Me Home, Country Roads," and my closest friends and players all locked arms around me. Just outside of that circle, many of the parents of my players stood by, smiling.

It was a beautiful moment I will never forget. These parents had trusted me not just with the responsibility of coaching their sons for the last six years but also with taking them on two trips abroad to America. They recognized my efforts, my passion, and my desire to impact their sons. They were also willing to overlook my many errors and mistakes as a young basketball coach. And now, along with their sons, they were there to say thank you. After that song, each athlete and parent lined up and took the time to let me know how much I meant to them.

When I look back on the hundreds of athletes I've coached, the ones with whom I have had the closest relationship and probably the greatest influence on, I also remember their parents. While they may not have been my primary point of contact, they've been close by, looking on, and a part of the biggest moments with their child. I am still in touch with many of these parents today, and my only regret is I didn't bring more parents closer.

That's what *the sports parent solution* is about—bringing the parents in your program a little closer to the circle of athletes and you.

WHAT'S NEXT?

Thank you for taking the time to read my book, *The Sports Parent Solution*. If you found it valuable, I would be grateful if you would consider writing a review online. Your review would go a long way toward encouraging other people to read the book, and it might even help your child's coach someday.

To leave a review, please visit www.tocculture.com/thesportsparentsolution.

If you have any questions, comments, or feedback, please feel free to contact me at jpnerbun@tocculture.com.

If you enjoyed *The Sports Parent Solution*, you may also like my book *The Culture System*, as well as my weekly articles. You can sign up for my newsletter at tocculture.com.

Finally, if you would like to learn more about the ideas in *The Sports Parent Solution*, I offer a number of resources:

- ➜ Book Club Discussion Guide
- ➜ Implementation Checklist
- ➜ Online Course

You can download these resources at:
www.tocculture.com/thesportsparentsolution.

ACKNOWLEDGMENTS

Shortly after the publication of *The Culture System*, I approached my wife, Melissa, to discuss my intention to embark on writing yet another book. The endeavor of writing a book is demanding not just for myself, but also for my family. Understandably, Melissa's initial response wasn't brimming with enthusiasm, but when I explained how it would be a book for coaches on working with parents, she was quickly behind it. Having been my steadfast companion through most of my encounters with sports parents, she comprehended the book's value not only to coaches but to their families as well. I am profoundly appreciative of her unwavering support throughout the creation of this latest work.

Second, I can't take sole credit for this book. I've been fortunate to have an incredible "Writing Team" comprised of coaches and athletic directors who read early drafts and provided invaluable feedback. Many of them generously shared their own successes, challenges, and mistakes. My writing team included:

Nate VanDuyne	Al Baker	Sam Klassen
Mark Cascio	Patrick Quirk	Kyle Rehrig
Andy Cerroni	Nick Pocius	Nathan Emerick
Dan Sullivan	Lance Knudson	Joe Willis
Colleen Dawson	Darryl Osborn	Joshua Strasser
Tyler Wright	Tyler Pearson	Erik Robitaille

Additionally, Nate Sanderson served as a content editor, fearlessly challenging me throughout the book and contributing his own compelling story and the foreword. Even more significantly, Nate has acted as a testing ground for many of these innovative strategies with his teams and parents over the years.

I'm profoundly grateful for the coaches I've supported in the TOC Community through 1:1 coaching and consulting. They placed their trust in me by embracing these strategies and demonstrating immense courage in their interactions with parents. I've translated their stories and insights into this book, and I value their openness to having their experiences shared.

Finally, I want to acknowledge my editor, Amanda Rooker, and her team at Split Seed Media for aiding me in overcoming my writing limitations. I'm thankful to collaborate with such a skilled editor and appreciate the attention and care they dedicated to this book.

ABOUT THE AUTHOR

J.P. Nerbun is a bestselling author, leadership coach, and founder of TOC Culture Consulting, a leading global sports-consulting and leadership coaching business. His mission is to support leaders and their teams to achieve their full potential through 1:1 coaching, consulting, and community.

Nerbun's impressive scope spans across sports, education, healthcare, and business, with a proven track record of guiding leaders at esteemed institutions such as Stanford University, Harvard University, University of Texas, the USGA, and Chick-Fil-A.

In 2019, he published his first book, *Calling Up: Discovering Your Journey to Transformational Leadership*, which has received critical acclaim. In 2022, he published *The Culture System*, a groundbreaking book offering a framework for developing team culture.

In 2023, he launched TOC Coaching and Culture Certification, which has been praised for being the most comprehensive online coach education available. His podcast, *Coaching Culture*, is one of the top sports leadership podcasts globally. Nerbun lives in Ireland with his wife and their three children.

Learn more at tocculture.com.

PRACTICAL COACH EDUCATION FOR TODAY'S SPORTING ENVIRONMENT

TOC Coaching & Culture Certification

Want to become a more transformational coach and build a great team culture? Learn The Culture System Framework at your own pace with this one-of-a-kind online training platform.

In this course, J.P. Nerbun will help you deepen your commitment to Transformational Coaching and teach you the proven methods, tools, and strategies of the best teams and organizations in the world. In this course, you'll get access to customizable digital tools and a group chat to engage with experienced coaches in the 4-part framework.

You'll be inspired and transformed through the stories and lessons of real leaders who've made changes in their leadership and successfully applied these methods and tools within their organizations.

ENDNOTES

1   J. P. Nerbun and Nate Sanderson, "Episode 255: Coaching Culture," *The Coaching Culture Podcast*, July 31, 2022, https://podcasts.apple.com/sk/podcast/255-cody-royle-part-1/id1286560192?i=1000574513779.

2   J. P. Nerbun, *The Culture System: A Proven Process for Creating an Extraordinary Team Culture* (TOC Culture Consulting, 2022).

3   Garland Cooper, "Coaches are leaving youth sports—and not for the reason you'd think," *USA Today*, June 13, 2017, https://usatodayhss.com/2017/coaches-are-leaving-youth-sports-and-not-for-the-reason-youd-think.

4   Richard Weissbourd, *The Parents We Mean to Be: How Well-Intentioned Adults Undermine Children's Moral and Emotional Development* (Houghton Mifflin Harcourt, 2009), 155.

5   Joe Ehrmann, *InSideOut Coaching* (Simon & Schuster, 2011), 129.

6   Ehrmann, *InSideOut Coaching*, 327.

7   Harvard Online, "Benefits of home visits by teachers," Youtube, youtube.com/watch?v=HDzCSNLT8Hw.

8   June Kronholz, "Teacher Home Visits," *Education Next* (Summer 2016), https://www.educationnext.org/wp-content/uploads/2022/03/ednext_XVI_3_kronholz.pdf.

9   Kronholz, "Teacher Home Visits."

10   Laura Meckler, "Public education is facing a crisis of epic proportions," *Washington Post*, January 30, 2022, https://www.washingtonpost.com/education/2022/01/30/public-education-crisis-enrollment-violence/.

11   Chip Heath and Dan Heath, *The Power of Moments: Why Certain Experiences Have Extraordinary Impact* (Corgi, 2019), 5.

12   Chris Voss, *Never Split the Difference: Negotiating as if Your Life Depended on It* (Harper Business, 2016), 25.

13   Carl J. Pierson, *The Politics of Coaching: A Survival Guide to Keep Coaches from Getting Burned* (Double Nickle Press, 2011).

14   Weissbourd, *The Parents We Mean to Be.*

15   Dr. Jane Nelsen, *Positive Discipline: The Classic Guide to Helping Children Develop Self-Discipline, Responsibility, Cooperation, and Problem Solving Skills* (Ballantine Books, 2006).

Printed in Great Britain
by Amazon

44802611R00106